IB PSYCHOLOGY
Internal Assessment

IB PSYCHOLOGY
Internal Assessment

The Definitive Psychology [HL/SL] IA
Guide For the International Baccalaureate [IB] Diploma

Lee Kwan

Zouev IB Diploma Publishing

This book is printed on acid-free paper.

Copyright © 2023 Zouev IB Diploma Publishing. All rights reserved.

No part of this book may be used or reproduced in any manner whatsoever without written permission, except in the case of brief quotations embodied in critical articles or reviews.

Published 2023

Printed by Zouev IB Diploma Publishing

ISBN 978-1-9163451-9-5, paperback.

TABLE OF CONTENTS

PART I THE IB PSYCHOLOGY IA GUIDE 9

    1. INTRODUCTION TO THE PSYCHOLOGY IA 10

    2. PLANNING YOUR PSYCHOLOGY IA 11

    3. WRITING YOUR PSYCHOLOGY IA 15

    4. THE ASSESSMENT CRITERIA 33

PART II   SEVEN EXAMPLES OF EXCELLENT IB PSYCHOLOGY IA 43

    1. EXAMPLE ONE (20/22) 45

    2. EXAMPLE TWO (22/22) 55

    3. EXAMPLE THREE (19/22) 67

    4. EXAMPLE FOUR (21/22) 79

    5. EXAMPLE FIVE (21/22) 85

    6. EXAMPLE SIX (19/22) 97

    7. EXAMPLE SEVEN (22/22) 107

PART I
THE IB PSYCHOLOGY IA GUIDE

1. INTRODUCTION TO THE PSYCHOLOGY IA

The Psychology Internal Assessment (IA) is one of the most challenging components of the IB for many students, however doing well in this IA requires you following very straightforward steps. By going very thoroughly and methodologically through the requirements of the IB criteria and this list of sentence-by-sentence guidance, you are definitely on your way to acing the Psych IA and getting that idolized 7. While these steps can be adjusted and more can be added to your own IA as this assignment is different for every student and study, I have tried to make each step as basic as possible so anyone can do well on their Psych IA (even if you have a bad teacher or are just very confused!)

I have spent many hours compiling together guidance for every section of the Psych IA, the appropriate amount of sentences and paragraphs for each section, and what they should individually cover and how. As such, I have split this guide into 2 parts, where one is <u>Planning Your Psychology IA</u> and the other is <u>Writing Your Psychology IA</u>. In the second part, the paragraphs and what to include in each are listed in chronological order. Therefore, they should be included in the order they are stated.

Disclaimer: This book is not written by an IB examiner or any professional, just a student who has gone through the IB and wants to help others get a good mark! To do so, I've looked at different resources that will help you if you are struggling to wrap your head around what exactly needs to be covered in the IA. It's not foolproof, but should be able to give you lots of guidance!

2. PLANNING YOUR PSYCHOLOGY IA

Finding the right time frame for your study:

Finding an experiment that no one else is doing and is clear enough to follow is always kind of difficult for any Psych student. You might stumble across studies that others are doing, or might find hyper specific studies with complicated terminology you've never seen before. One of the main issues I came across when writing my IA was the age of the study. I recommend that you **find a recent study** rather than one done before the 1980s, for example. Chances are, more recent studies have plenty of valid theory behind it and the methodology that you can follow is much more precise than older studies.

I had a study for my Psych IA that was pretty much a pioneer in its field and was conducted in the 1970s. This meant there was virtually no preceding theory or studies, and the researchers couldn't really compare itself to other research in the paper. This proved to be an issue that could have easily been curbed if we'd just looked at recent, simpler studies on well-known phenomena with lots of theory behind it already.

Knowing what statistical testing was used:

The study my IA was based on was one where the 'sign test' was used and this is not a good testing method for IA writing students. It requires a specific type of environment with certain results from your study, and isn't a *robust method* to analyse data with.

Each statistical test that's created is an improvement from the previous ones, and this is a very old test. Therefore, **try to stick with studies using the well-known "t-test"** so you don't have to worry about this being a problem when you yourself try to compare results and are forced to use another statistical technique.

Understanding the theoretical background:

You will be marked according to your **connection** of the study you've found to a specific named theoretical background and further the replication you plan to do. Therefore, you should introduce them in the given order below.

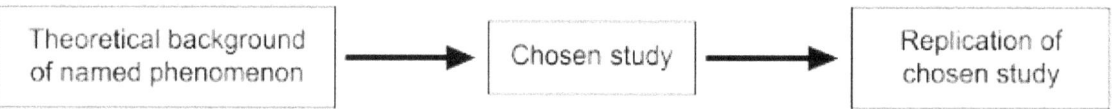

Understanding that being able to make this connection between the 3 main elements of your study requires you first fully grasping what **theory** the chosen study is based on. If you find a really old study (ie. one from the 1950s), it might not be based on theory but may actually be *generating* theory. This will be difficult to discuss in terms of theoretical *context* since it didn't really exist before that study took place.

One of the fundamental things to understand from this point is that **you must have a clear "theory" stated in your IA that is linked to your chosen study, and thus your replication.** If your study, for some reason, does not have a clear theory behind it, try to avoid it and look for something with a clearly stated heuristic or bias, for example.

What to do before conducting the study

Here are some major things every Psych student needs to consider when doing the replication once they've figured out what study they're going to replicate.

Writing a list of ALL materials you will use

Before starting, gather together with your group and **meticulously plan every step of how you will use ALL materials needed.** This includes props (ie. basketballs, presentations, recorded audio) and regular materials (ie. computers, pens, chairs, etc.).

This is to ensure that, if your group needs to be split amongst classes to conduct the experiment, every one of you use the *exact same materials*. You can use this act of controlling the standardisation of researchers' procedure for every condition/group as a strength in your study. This is discussed in the evaluation section below.

Write a step-by-step tutorial for EVERY step of your study

There is a section later in the IA where you need to list, in super simple words and numbered steps, how you conducted experiment (Section 3: Exploration). This should be so clear that any person reading your IA should be able to conduct the study in the exact same way without missing any step. Before you start, gather your group to create this step-by-step tutorial including every stage of your experiment. Not only does this make your job 10x easier later on, you've also completed 1 whole section for your IA without having even done the study yet.

Brainstorm how you will gather participants:

You will have to communicate with teachers and students to be able to get participants for your study. You need to sort out:

- how many participants you need.

- how many conditions you need for your chosen experimental design.

- which classes you can/can't interrupt.

- what times your group can do the study during the school day.

- which teachers you need to communicate with in advance about what time suits them.

Your group needs to look at potential classes they can interrupt and discuss with the class's teacher what time would suit them best. You can't barge into a class and start the experiment, even if that sounds tempting and time-saving!

Clearly identify your IV* and DV:**

*IV=Independent Variable

**DV=Dependent Variable

Understanding WHAT you are actually manipulating is **crucial** to your IA. You need to make it very clear what is the 1 thing you are changing, and what is the thing that will be affected. Many students skip this step, and this costs them once they sit down, start writing their IA and finally realise that what they were testing is not what they are **claiming** they're studying. If you get caught in this trap, you will lose points.

3. WRITING YOUR PSYCHOLOGY IA

Title Page:

Title: Psychology Internal Assessment

Subtitle: Focus of your own study

Word count:

This should not be more than 2000 words and excludes:

- Title page
- References
- Section headings
- Parenthetical citations
- Graphs
- Appendices

Session you will do your final exams (ie. May 2020)

Your personal code

Personal codes of other students in your group

Here's an example of what your Psych IA Title Page could look like:

Psychology Internal Assessment

Lorem ipsum dolor sit amet, consectetur adipiscing elit.

Word count: 2150
May 2020
Personal code: hqt335
Other group members: hqt115, hqt265, hqt167

1ˢᵀ Section: Table of Contents:

This includes the page numbers for:

- table of contents (optional but preferred)

- introduction

- exploration

- analysis

- evaluation

- works cited

- include individual page numbers for each appendix

You should always keep in mind these change continually when you edit the document, so you need to regularly check the correct page numbers are being used in the table of contents. If this isn't followed up on at multiple points of the process (especially at the end), there's a chance you could lose easy points for organisation.

This can look something like this:

Table of contents

Table of contents	2
Introduction	3
Exploration	6
Analysis	8
Evaluation	10
Works cited	13
Appendix 1: Letter of consent	14
Appendix 2: Standardised instructions	16
Appendix 3: Participant questionnaire	17
Appendix 4: Lorem ipsum dolor sit amet, consectetur adipiscing elit	18
Appendix 5: Lorem ipsum dolor sit amet, consectetur adipiscing elit	19
Appendix 6: Lorem ipsum dolor sit amet, consectetur adipiscing elit	20
Appendix 7: Lorem ipsum dolor sit amet, consectetur adipiscing elit	21

2ⁿᵈ Section – Introduction:

This section is meant to provide an overview of what study you've chosen, what the theoretical background behind the original study is, and what your replicated study will be like. Talking about the theory and original study should be in **past tense.** When you talk about your replication of the study, this should be written in **future tense** as you *will be* conducting the study. Even if you've already done the replicated study, this should still be in future tense.

1st paragraph:

You need to briefly **explain the theory** your chosen study is based on.

2nd paragraph:

You should explicitly **connect the theory to the study** you've chosen

3rd longer paragraph:

In this paragraph, you should be giving the reader insight into *what* the study is about, and what it concluded. This should include a brief explanation of

- why you chose this specific study
- what happens inside original study in very basic detail
- results from original study

4th paragraph:

The 4th paragraph is finally the section you talk about your own replication of the chosen study. This should include:

- **1 sentence** stating explicitly **what you aim to determine** in your replicated study

- **1-2 sentences** stating clearly the IV and DV of your replication

5th paragraph:

This paragraph should be an opportunity to demonstrate "why this replication of the original study is important" in around **3-5 sentences**. Think of this as an exercise to show "what's the point of all of this? Why bother?" The most essential but more 'fancy' question that professional researchers would ask themselves is "What could this replication do for scientific research within psychology? What could this possibly give us? Why invest the time and money into doing this?"

If you're not sure *why* your replication is "important", fear not. Basically, no Psych student really knows why except to complete the dreaded task of a Psych IA. Unfortunately, though, you gotta think like a real psychology researcher and come up with a legitimate reason for doing this study.

To help you figure this out, consider how the following concepts might be different in the original study and your replicated study:

- the **timeframe** the original study was done in. If it was done long ago, are there certain things that may be different nowadays that may influence how participants respond to the same experiment?

- the **cultural context** of the original study and how that's different from your own

- the **difference in age** between the participants of the original study and IB students
    - you could talk about how replicating the original study with teenagers/international students/academically motivated people might provide insight into _____

- the **gender** of the participants in the original study versus those in your replication

- **technological differences** between the original study and your replication (would exposure to technology yield different results, or do the results also stand in this different setting as well (this is known as *transferability)*

- think about if the experiment originally conducted was **highly artificial**. Consider how the artificial nature of the study could have influenced the results, and how replicating your study in a more natural environment, like a classroom, is beneficial (again, this is referring to transferability)

In my own Psych IA, I stated that replication of the original study was important since the original study is very old. Therefore, we want to test if the results stand the test of time generally (in that testing this heuristic *using the method they did* is still a valid method). Additionally, we also said that, based on this, the exposure of teenagers to certain named influences (such as mobile phones and television) may be different than the original sample in the timeframe they did the test. This is because, in the 1970s, there wasn't such massive exposure to technological devices as there is today, and this could influence major elements of the study. This is known as the *temporal validity* of the study, and is good to use as a reason for replication for very old studies (like my own).

6th paragraph:

This is a short paragraph where 2 **essential** sentences are included:

- **1 sentence** clearly stating the research hypothesis. In this sentence, you should clearly identify clearly the IV and DV stated earlier

- **1 sentence** clearly stating the null hypothesis

3rd Section – Exploration:

This section is meant to detail the steps you took to conduct your replicated study from start to finish.

1st paragraph:

This is a paragraph that sets the scene for the reader. It is used so that you can go through the basic structural details of your study before you actually conducted it.

This must include:

- **1 sentence** must name what **research design** was used and what this means in terms of your study. For instance, you need to name that you used *independent samples design,* where participants were put into 2 groups and assigned to different conditions.

- **2 sentences**, explain what your **conditions** to test your variables are. If you have independent samples:
    - 1 sentence would be used to explain exactly what your *experimental condition* is
    - 1 sentence would be used to explain exactly what your *control condition* is

- **1 sentence** clearly stating the type of **sampling method** you chose and who the **participants** are. Most often students use *opportunity sampling of IB students aged between specified ages.*

- **1 sentence** stating where these participants were gathered from (ie. 3 pre-existing groups attending different English classes).

Why I included the term "pre-existing" is that there may be certain characteristics you can discuss later about how these groups may have varied abilities within English, for instance. If your replicated study is about spelling, then this is vital in understanding how *sampling biases* may have influenced your results due to your participants belonging to predetermined groups with potentially different levels of knowledge of English.

2nd paragraph:

This paragraph is made up of **4-7 sentences,** which are meant to explain if there were certain **measures you undertook to replicate certain key elements of the study**. Make this process clear and separate for the different conditions of your study, with the experimental condition(s) coming first and control(s) coming second, if you have controls.

In my own Psych IA, this was a paragraph explaining how we created a presentation of famous peoples' faces, wherein everything from timing to the audio we recorded to the specific faces we chose were justified with explicit explanations.

Ideally include **1 sentence** explaining if you did a **pilot study,** for what reason, and how this may have influenced your official replicated study. If you did one or multiple pilot studies and some came up with insignificant or unusable results (like in my own Psych IA), these don't need to be included.

3rd and 4th paragraph:

As mentioned earlier, you should have created a very basic and clear step-by-step tutorial as to how you did each part of the study. At the beginning, keep this step-by-step tutorial explicit and slowly cut down on the absolutely non-essential elements to it. Keeping as much as possible of your steps is important, but you also can't afford to use too many words explaining what you did. Therefore, cut any "fluffy" phrases and try to combine sentences where you can.

You also need to include basic materials used in ALL Psych IA studies. This includes reference to giving and receiving the **Consent Forms**, reading or handing out **Standardised Instructions**, and reference to a **Debrief** being given to participants. All documents referenced in this section must be put in the Appendix at the end of your IA. Therefore, when you mention any in this section, they must be labelled by what Appendix number the person reading your IA can look at to know what you're talking about.

- When you reference the first piece of material, you can reference it in this way: *The participants returned their consent forms (see Appendix 1).*

- Once you've referenced your first appendix, you can just include the appendix without "see" as this is now understood by the researcher after it came up the first time: *The participants were debriefed (Appendix 5).*

4th Section – Analysis:

(this is relevant if you see a few responses/results that deviate massively from everyone else)

- **1 sentence** would be used to explain **why** you used outlier analysis

- **1-2 sentences** explaining **how** outlier analysis was conducted. To do so, my group found a math tutorial for statistics students and explained briefly how we followed it.

Include your 1st Table

This table should be labelled something like "Table 1: Descriptive analysis of data" above it. This table should show the most crucial parts of the data from your study. This usually includes the **mean (M)** and the **standard deviation (SD)** for each of your conditions, as well as other relevant data if necessary. Keep in mind that *every piece of data presented in the table must be discussed*, which means using extra words. Therefore, try to include only the most important data values.

The table MUST follow the APA citation guide for tables.

Paragraph underneath Table 1

State the differences between data values (ie. the mean in one condition may be a bit lower than the other condition). If there is a difference in standard deviation, you can talk about the fact there is *greater variance* in the responses of participants to the different conditions. Therefore, you could state that in one condition, participants may have been more unsure than in the other of how to respond, for instance. Try look at your own study, and try explain what could possibly cause the spread of responses to be larger in one condition. In every point and statement you make, explicitly state the numbers seen in the table.

Include your 1st figure

This figure show the most important comparison of data (ie. different mean responses in each condition). Creating this figure must follow APA guidelines and usually is shown using a bar chart as this is super clear for the reader. However, this can be also done with a line chart or something similar if that's more appropriate for your study.

To create this graph, you don't need anything fancy. Both Microsoft Excel and Google Sheets have good, clear chart making programs that are used most commonly by IB students every year.

Paragraph underneath figure

This is a paragraph that is meant to analyse the table and figure shown above. This should include:

- **1 sentence** stating you conducted a certain statistical test (most commonly used among IB students is the "t-test") and what it was used to compare.

  For example, "*An independent samples t-test was conducted to compare _____ in the experimental condition and _____ in the control condition.*" A very good and commonly used t-test website calculator is VassarStats. You just plug in the raw data of your 2 conditions (if you're using independent samples) and it generates all you need for this paragraph. Look at this website with your Psych teacher if you're confused about what the different terms mean as there are **many** different calculations done on the website so it can initially be confusing.

- **1 sentence** stating if there was a statistically significant difference in data in conditions or not.

In essence, this statement should look something like this:

"*The t-test showed there was **(not) a significant** difference in the responses for those in the experimental condition **(M=?, SD=?)** and those in the control condition **(M=?, SD=?); t(?)=?, p=?.***"

If p-value is smaller than 0.01, your results are considered significant. If you have *statistically significant* results, you can state that **you are *able to reject* the null hypothesis**. If you have *statistically insignificant* results, you can state that **you are *not able to reject* the null hypothesis.**

Don't give up at this point if you have statistically insignificant results! This does not mean your hard work went to waste or that what you initially thought about your study was wrong. There are still many things you can talk about in terms of the mean and standard deviation if there are interesting differences! :)

- **1 sentence** stating what accepting/rejecting the null hypothesis means *in terms of your actual study.* You can start the sentence with something like "This means that..." or "That is, it appears..."

5th Section – Evaluation:

This section primarily covers what you found out about your study and gives you the opportunity to look at how it's different from and similar to the original study. Not only that, but it acts as a time for you to reflect on what you could've done better and what could be done in future research to counter any limitations you came across.

1st paragraph

This paragraph should provide an overview of what your analysis and findings means in terms of your study. This should include

- **1 sentence** stating if your results do or don't support the original study's findings. Supporting the original study doesn't necessarily mean you need to have a significant p-value, but it can be shown through similar trends in terms of the mean and standard deviation.
- **1 sentence** stating the p-value of the original study
- **1 sentence** stating what this meant in terms of the study
- **1 sentence** comparing the p-value of the original study to your own p-value
    - if your results are statistically insignificant, include 1 sentence referencing the mean/standard deviation and how either or both of these might still support the original study's findings

2nd and 3rd paragraph

These paragraphs are meant to summarise key strengths and limitations in your study. These can be due to your own actions as researchers or may naturally occur.

- **2-3 identified strengths** in your study and with each identified strength, 1 sentence explaining in what way this strength was created or how it positively impacted your study. This can refer to using *pilot studies*, usage of *standardised intervals* between certain parts of the study, *controls* for specific biases, etc.
- **2-3 identified major limitations** in your study and with each identified limitation, 1 sentence explaining in what way this strength was weakened your study. This can refer to using not controlling for specific **relevant** *biases*, issues with the *sample*, etc.

For *each* limitation, come up with 1 **realistic potential solution** that could've been implemented in future research.

As a general note, ideally intertwine the strengths and limitations. This will demonstrate an in-depth understanding of your study. Intertwining can be done through identifying 1 element of your study, like the study's sample. You can find 1 strength and 1 limitation in using the specific sample you had and how these could have influenced the results of the study.

IMPORTANT! You should identify strengths and limitations by covering different parts of your IA equally. This includes making reference to your **sampling technique**, what kind of **participants** you gathered, the **materials** you used, and the **experimental design** you used.

4th paragraph

This paragraph is meant to be an opportunity to summarise your most important findings and wrap your IA up. In this paragraph, you should include:

- **1 sentence** stating that you can/can't reject the null hypothesis
- **1 sentence** stating what this result means in terms of your study
- **1 sentence** stating a concluding statement starting with something like "From this study, we can conclude that..."

6th Section – Works Cited:

This section includes all the works you referenced, theory your study is based on and where possible images/names/letters you've used are from. These need to be done in APA style (American Psychological Association) and in alphabetical order.

7th Section – Appendices:

What to include:

In this section, you need to include all documents and material shown to participants. This includes things such as your debrief, standardised instructions, and consent form. Along with this, your study will most likely include showing certain materials (such as faces, lists of letters, pictures, etc.) and these also need to be included in the appendices. Essentially, anyone wanting to do your study exactly the same way again should be able to look at this section and have every piece of material specific to the study available to them.

The appendix must also include screenshots of the statistical calculator you used to arrive at your results seen in Section 4: Analysis. I took screenshots of my results in the t-test used on the VassarStats website. I took screenshots of ALL of the page with the results included.

You need to include raw data for each condition as well in this section. This refers to all of the numbers that look a bit complicated and messy that you based your results on. Put this into clear-ish tables so anyone reading the IA can still get a gist of what the numbers are meant to refer to.

What order do the appendices go in?

Order the appendices according to the order in which they are mentioned in Section 3: Exploration. If there are materials not mentioned in the section, include them after the named appendices in whatever order seems most logical to you.

What happens if one of my appendices overlap into multiple pages?

No stress, if your material (such as screenshots of your t-test) go over 2-3 pages, you don't need to make your appendix super small to fit into 1 page. Make sure that each page of this section only has the information of 1 appendix. This means there should be ***no pages where 2 or more appendices overlap.*** Here's what you should avoid:

By looking at this document, you can see that 2 different appendices are included on 1 page. Don't do this!

Instead of doing this, you should instead separate all of you appendices even if it makes your IA very long. It makes your information very clear to anyone reading the IA, and if you don't do this you could lose easy points for organisation. Here's what you should be doing with appendices:

Appendices
Appendix 1: Letter of consent

Lorem ipsum dolor sit amet, consectetur adipiscing elit. Cras ipsum quam, tincidunt eu neque vitae, consectetur venenatis sapien. Aenean eu risus volutpat venenatis dapibus eu dictum eget odio.

Duis eleifend lorem et erat pulvinar sollicitudin. Duis rutrum:

- Quisque tempor neque eget lorem euismod lacinia. Aenean ac maximus eros. Sed ac euismod risus, nec imperdiet eros.
- Nullam ex sapien, pulvinar eget sapien nec blandit ornare risus.
- Class aptent taciti sociosqu ad litora torquent per conubia nostra, per inceptos himenaeos.

Aliquam eget felis feugiat, porttitor diam sed, sollicitudin diam. Etiam eget ipsum eget massa tincidunt imperdiet.

I, _____ cras volutpat lacinia eros at fermentum. Vestibulum porttitor, est eget venenatis aliquet, metus nisi porta sapien, eget facilisis urna risus id lorem.

Donec ac purus fringilla, auctor diam ultrices, sodales diam. Praesent tincidunt sit amet diam in euismod. Sed consectetur posuere est nec ornare.

Signature: _____   Date: _____

Parental signature: _____   Date: _____

Appendix 2: Standardised instructions

Welcome, and thank you for participating in our experiment.

[Lorem ipsum placeholder text]

Any questions?

If you follow all of these steps from start to finish, you should be well on your way to getting a 7 in your Psych IA!

4. THE ASSESSMENT CRITERIA

IB PSYCHOLOGY HL
(Internal Assessment Criteria)

Name (s) _____

A   Introduction

Marks	Level Descriptor
0	• There is no introduction or the background research presented is not made relevant to the experimental hypothesis. • The aim of the study is not stated. • No hypotheses are stated.
1 - 3	• Background theories and/or studies are identified but are limited in number, not well explained and/or not highly relevant to the hypotheses. • The aim of the study is clearly stated. • The experimental and or null hypotheses are stated but are unclear or not operationalized. • The prediction made in the experimental hypothesis is not clearly justified by the background studies and/or theories.
4 - 5	• Background theories and/or studies are adequately explained and highly relevant to the hypotheses. • The aim of the study is clearly stated. • The experimental and null hypotheses are appropriately stated and operationalized. • The prediction made in the experimental hypothesis is justified by the background studies and/or theories.

COMMENTS:

B   Method: Design

Marks	Level Descriptor
0	- The independent variable and dependent variable are not accurately identified. - No appropriate experimental design is identified. - There is no evidence of appropriate application of ethical guidelines, for example, there is no evidence that informed consent was obtained from participants or their parents.
1	- The independent variable and dependent variable are accurately identified but not operationalized. - The experimental design is appropriate to the aim of the research but its selection has not been appropriately justified. - There is a clear indication and documentation of how ethical guidelines were followed.
2	- The independent variable and dependent variable are accurately identified and operationalized. - The experimental design is appropriate to the aim and its use is appropriately justified. - There is clear indication and documentation of how ethical guidelines were followed.

COMMENTS:

C Method: Participants

Marks	Level Descriptor
0	- No relevant characteristics of the participants are identified. - No relevant sampling technique is identified or the sampling method is incorrectly identified. - The target population has not been identified.
1	- Some characteristics of the participants are identified but not all are relevant. Some relevant participant characteristics have been omitted. - The sample is selected using an appropriate method but the use of the method is not explained. - The target population has been identified and is appropriate.
2	- Relevant characteristics of the participants are identified. - The sample is selected using an appropriate method and the use of this method is explained. - The target population has been identified and is appropriate.

COMMENTS:

D   Method: Procedure

Marks	Level Descriptor
0	• No relevant procedural information is included. • The information provided does not allow replication. • There are no details of how the ethical guidelines were applied.
1	• The procedural information is relevant but not clearly described, so that the study is not easily replicable. • Details of how the ethical guidelines were applied are included. • Necessary materials have not been included and referenced in the appendices.
2	• The procedural information is relevant and clearly described, so that the study is easily replicable. • Details of how the ethical guidelines were applied are included. • Necessary materials have been included and referenced in the appendices.

COMMENTS:

E Results: Descriptive

Marks	Level Descriptor
0	• There are no results or the results are irrelevant to the stated hypotheses of the student's experimental study. • Relevant descriptive statistics have not been applied to the data. • There is no graphing of the data.
1	• Results are inaccurate and do not reflect the hypotheses of the research. • Descriptive statistics (one measure of central tendency and one measure of dispersion) are applied to the data, but their use is not explained. • The graph of results is not accurate, is unclear or is not sufficiently related to the hypotheses of the study. • Results are not presented in both words and tabular form.
2	• Results are clearly stated and accurate and reflect the hypotheses of the research. • Appropriate descriptive statistics (one measure of central tendency and one measure of dispersion) are applied to the data and their use is explained. • The graph of results is accurate, clear and directly relevant to the hypotheses of the study. • Results are presented on both words and tabular form.

COMMENTS:

F   Results: Inferential

Marks	Level Descriptor
0	- No appropriate inferential statistical test has been applied.
1	- An appropriate inferential statistical test has been chosen but not properly applied
2	- An appropriate inferential statistical test has been chosen and explicitly justified. - Results of the inferential statistical test are not complete or may be poorly stated.
3	- An appropriate inferential statistical test has been chosen and explicitly justified. - Results of the inferential statistical test are accurately stated. - The null hypothesis has been *accepted* or rejected appropriately according to the results of the statistical test. - A statement of statistical significance is appropriate and clear.

COMMENTS:

G   Discussion

Marks	Level Descriptor
0	- There is no discussion section, or the discussion of the results is irrelevant to the hypotheses.
1 - 2	- Discussion of the results is very superficial. - The findings of the student's experimental study are not compared to the study being replicated. - Limitations of the design and procedure are not accurately identified. - No modifications are suggested and there is not conclusion.
3 - 5	- Discussion of the results is not well developed or is incomplete (for example, discussion of either the descriptive or inferential statistics is missing). - The findings of the student's experimental study are mentioned with reference to relevant background studies and/or theories. - Some relevant limitations of the design and procedure have been identified, but a rigorous analysis method is not achieved. - Some modifications are suggested. - The conclusion is appropriate.
6 - 8	- Discussion of results is well developed and complete (for example, descriptive and inferential statistics are discussed). - The findings of the student's experimental study are discussed with reference to relevant background studies and/or theories. - Limitations of the design and procedure are highly relevant and have been rigorously analyzed. - Modifications are suggested and ideas for further research are mentioned. - The conclusion is appropriate.

COMMENTS:

H   Citation of Sources

Marks	Level Descriptor
0	• Sources are not cited within the report. • No references are provided, or no standard citation method is used.
1	• The references are incomplete **or** a standard citation method is not used consistently.
2	• All in-text citations and references are provided. • A standard citation method is used consistently throughout the body of the report and in the references section.

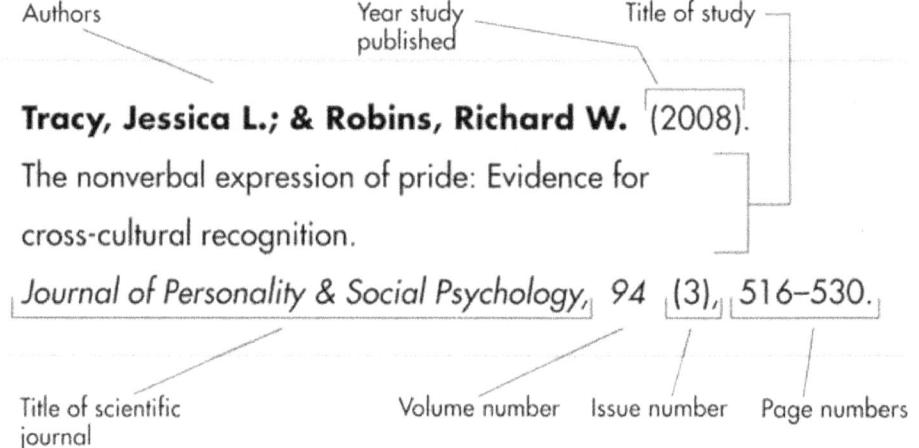

COMMENTS:

I Report Format

Marks	Level Descriptor
0	• The report is not within the word limit of 1,500-2,000 words. • Required sections of the report are missing, for example, no abstract is included. • Appendices are missing or incomplete.
1	• The report is within the word limit of 1,500-2,000 words. • The report is complete but not in the required format. • Appendices are not labeled appropriately and/or are not referenced in the body of the report. • The abstract is poorly written and does not include a summary overview of the student's experimental study, including the results.
2	• The report is within the word limit of 1,500-2,000 words. • The report is complete and in the required format. • Appendices are labeled appropriately and are referenced in the body of the report. • The abstract is clearly written and includes a summary overview of the student's experimental study, including the results.

COMMENTS:

PART II
SEVEN EXAMPLES OF EXCELLENT IB PSYCHOLOGY IA

The IA featured in this section are all recently submitted IA that scored exceptionally well (band 7) after being moderated by the IBO. The IA are presented in the exact same way as they were submitted, without any edits or changes to formatting. We do not retain the copyright of these IA, nor is this publication endorsed by the IBO. The Internal Assessments are being re-printed with the permission of the original authors.

1. EXAMPLE ONE (20/22)

Title: An Investigation of Mismatched Visual Interference in Serial Verbal Reactions

Author: Anonymous

Session: May 2020

Level: HL

Table of Contents

Section	Pages
Introduction	2-3
Exploration	3-4
Analysis	5-6
Evaluation	6-8
References	9
Appendices	9-14

An individual's ability to verbally react to a stimulus can be challenged by many factors. This idea has given rise to many studies that explore conflicting stimuli. Original studies in this field, although related to interference, did not focus on mismatched stimuli and studied how practice and repeated exposure to the same stimuli would create associations to give faster responses and how difficult it was for the individual to adjust to a new task if the response required was altered. J. Ridley Stroop studied the interference of mismatched stimuli and a psychological affect was named after him thanks to his research lead, the Stroop effect, which demonstrates that there is a delayed reaction to a task due to an interference of a mismatching stimulus. The most common example of this which demonstrates the effect is the 'Stroop Test', which asks participants to name the colour of a word and suggests that it takes longer and that there will be more errors when naming a colour if it is printed in a mismatched colour than if it is printed in the congruent colour. Stroop carried out a study at the George Peabody College in 1935 and explored why individuals could read out a colour faster than they could name it and *"interference in serial verbal reactions"*. Three different experiments all related to the effect of interferences on the ability to name colours serially were carried out, but the interference differed in every experiment. While the first experiment studied on the effects of interfering colour stimuli, the second experiment focused on effects of interfering word stimuli and the last studied the 'effects of practice upon interference'.

For this Internal Assessment, we only replicated the first experiment, where two colour tests were created, one printed in black and one printed in different colours that would pose as the interfering stimulus. The aim of the research was to determine whether the influence of a mismatch in colour would increase the time taken to read out names of colours from a 100-word list.

Independent Variable: whether the name of the colour was written in a mismatched (incongruent) colour or in black ink.
Dependent Variable: the time taken in seconds for the participants to read out each list of 100 words.

The null hypothesis: When reading a list of 100 colour names there will be no significant difference between the time taken in seconds if names of colours printed in black and the time taken to read a list of names of colours printed in incongruent (mismatched) colours and that any difference in the time taken is due to chance.

Alternative hypothesis: the average time taken, in seconds, to read a list of 100 names of colours is significantly longer when naming names of colours printed in mismatched ink.

EXPLORATION

In this replication of the study, we used a repeated measures design, so all participants took part in every condition of the independent variable. This was done to minimise the participant variables, because statistical differences in the results can be established more easily. The sample of participants was made up of twenty 15-18-year-old IB students from different cultural backgrounds all attending the British School of Warsaw, 9 female and 11 males. Despite cultural differences all spoke fluent English. Opportunity sampling was used, since it was the least time consuming and convenient. The IB1 Psychology class was asked to participate in the experiment.

The materials used for the experiment consisted of three lists of 100 words. Each list consisted of 5 words *(blue, green, red, purple and brown)* and each was printed 20 times. The first list of words was printed in black (Appendix 5). The key control variables were measures taken to avoid regularity in the list of colour names. For, the second list of words consisted of the first list but was printed in mismatched ink which also consisted of the five colours (Appendix 6). The colours were chosen based on the colours used in Stroop's original study. Colours like yellow and orange were not used since there is difficulty in reading yellow and orange is too similar to red. All lists were printed in the same font and size with double spacing in order to avoid possible confounding variables relating to the printing style. The lists had each word was typed twice in each row and column, every colour was used twice in each row, no colour name was be printed the corresponding colour, and no colour name was immediately repeated in either column or row. Furthermore, participants were taking the tests individually and conversation between participants was prohibited.

The procedure of the experiment was as follows:

1. Materials such as the 100-word lists, briefing and debriefing forms and all other materials were prepared beforehand.
2. Consent forms (Appendix 1) were given to all participants and they were asked to bring a signed copy for the day of the experiment.
3. Next, participants were briefed (Appendix 2) and were given standardized instructions (Appendix 4) informing them on the procedures of the experiments.
4. The sample of participants was split into two groups (Group 1 and Group 2) through random allocation by allowing individuals to randomly pick out a '1' or a '2' from a container.
5. Consent forms were collected, and the two groups were briefed and the standardized instructions (Appendix 3) were read to the participants.
6. Two classrooms were prepared in which an individual from each group would take the test.
7. Individuals were asked to read out two list of words under timed conditions and to make corrections when mistakes were made, while one researcher was recording the time taken to read the 100 words and the other researcher was recording how many mistakes were made.
8. Participants were asked not to discuss the experiment with other participants after having completed the tests
9. This procedure was repeated so many times until every participant had taken the every test.
10. All participants were debriefed and told that the experiment was now over.

Results (Descriptive)

The data obtained was interval data was also obtained, since the time taken to read each list was recorded. The raw data table and the mean time taken can be found in the Appendices (Appendix 7&8). The table below shows the mean and standard deviation results based on the raw data.

	List 1 – printed in black ink	List 2 – printed in mismatched ink
Overall mean time to read List of words (seconds)	53,40	52,42
Standard deviation	18,48	12,17

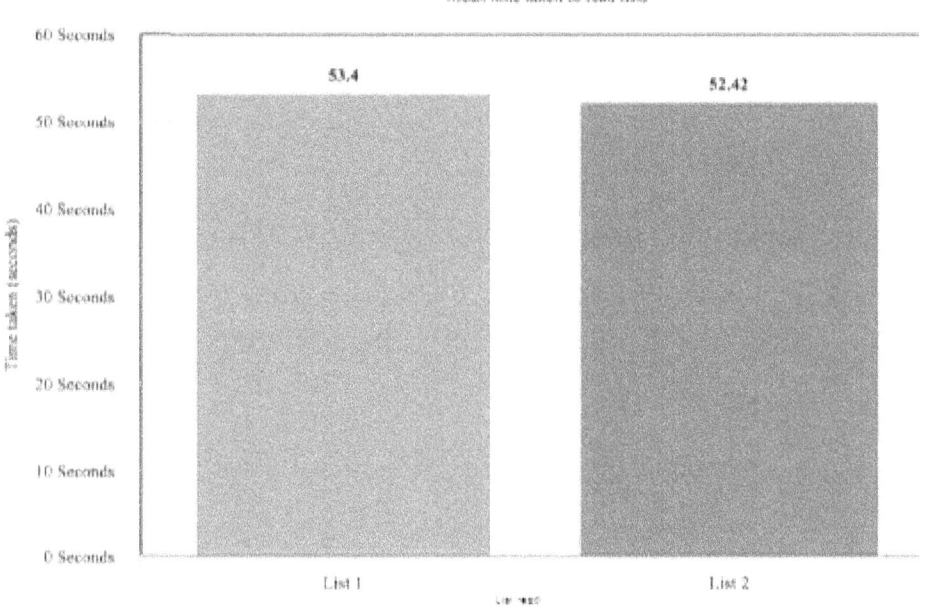

Mean time taken to read lists

The results of the study (Raw Data – Appendix 7) show that the mean time taken for females to read List 1 (58,42 seconds) was longer than the mean time taken to read List 2 (52,49 seconds), whereas the mean number of mistakes made when reading the list significantly increased from 1,38 in List 1 to 2,78 in List 2. On the other hand, the mean time taken for males to read List 1 (49,29 seconds) was shorter than the mean time taken to read List 2 (52,01 seconds), while only a small change in the mean number of mistakes made occurred, at a mean number of 2,36 and 2,40 mistakes made, respectively.

Inferential

T-TEST: to test the significance of the differences between time taken to read lists and to see whether it was correlational or by chance. Using the t-test helps researchers determine whether the differences in the results are big enough for the results to belong to distinct different groups, while also investigating variability of the scores, or the standard error. The t-test is a suitable method based on the design of this study and the two groups of data that were obtained.

P value and statistical significance:

P value: .8044

Confidence interval:

Mean time taken for List 1 – mean time taken for List 2 = 0.9785

95% confidence interval at this difference: between -7.1754 and 9.1324

Values from calculations:

$t = 0.243$ (Formula used - Appendix 9)

Standard error of difference = 3.896

Since this p-value is higher than .05, it shows that this difference is considered to be statistically insignificant. Therefore, we must accept the null hypothesis. This suggests that there is no significant impact of the colour that names of words are printed in on the time taken to read a list of 100 colour names.

EVALUATION

The experiment failed to show that the average time taken to read the list of 100 words is significantly longer when naming names of colours printed in mismatched ink. The mean time taken to read List 1 was 53.40 seconds which is longer than the mean time taken to read List 2 which only took 52.42

seconds. Although, there was a difference between males and females, since males took 2,72 seconds longer to read List 2 than List 1, while females were 5,93 seconds faster at reading List 1. This does not support the hypothesis of the experiment. However, the mean number of mistakes made when reading the lists of words increased with both samples, thus suggesting that the mismatched ink made it more difficult for participants to read the list of words, supporting the idea that the mismatched visual interference slows serial verbal reactions. In Stroop's original study, the overall mean time taken to read List 1 was 41,00 seconds, and the mean time taken to read list 2 was 43,30 seconds. Thus, it took 2,30 seconds longer to read the list of 100 words when printed in a mismatched colour, while in this replication, the overall mean time to read list 2 was 58 seconds faster than the mean time taken to read list 1.

There are various strengths of a repeated measures design. Participant variables are reduced since the same participants take part in each condition, including differences in factors such as IQ, language ability, age, etc. This also leads to more statistical power since variability between participants is controlled. Additionally, fewer participant are needed since every individual takes part in every condition.

Key limitations include order effects, so the changing performance of participants as a result of the order of the exposure to the different conditions, including the practice effect, the possibility that participants improve due to practice and become familiar with the task, or the fatigue effect, a gradual fall in concentration because of boredom, which could lead to a decrease in performance. However, the impact of order effects may be reduced using counterbalancing.[1] If half of the participants are exposed to the control condition first and then experimental condition, while the other half of participants is exposed first to the experimental condition and then to the control condition, the results should be less affected by order effects.

Additional strengths of this study include using standardized instructions since differences between the understanding of the procedure of the study were prevented. However, although participants were

[1] Field (2011)

asked not to communicate with one another, there was no supervisor. If the test was discussed, participants who have not yet carried out the tests could exhibit demand characteristics including expectancy effect where a participant knows what the researcher is expecting from the participant and thus acting accordingly.

Although opportunity sampling is convenient to the researcher as it is time efficient and individual differences between participants such as age and English ability were limited, it reduces the generalizability of the findings since it is not representative of society because of differences in age, social groups, education, etc. A modification to this could be carrying out research on a larger scale with greater variations within the group of participants that is more representative of different ages, cultures, IQ levels, etc.

Possible future research could be conducted on visual interference in serial verbal reactions on how the font the lists are printed in impact serial verbal reaction; the effect of other disfluency could be measured such as a list being written in bold, italic or underlined; or the effect of the colour of the paper/screen the list of words is displayed on.

In conclusion, the findings show that in this replication of Stroop's study, printing a list of colour names in mismatched colour print does not have a significant impact on the change in the time taken to read the list of 100 words. Although it took males 2.72 seconds longer to read the list of words printed in mismatched ink, the overall mean results show that it took 58 seconds longer to read the first list compared to the second list.

REFERENCES

Bergström, J. A., The relation of the interference of the practice effect of an association. *Amer. J. Psychol.*

Culler, A. J., Interference and adaptability. *Arch. of Psychol.*

J. Ridley Stroop (1935) Classics in the History of Psychology, Studies of Interference in serial verbal reactions. Christopher D. Green, York University, Toronto, Ontario.
http://psychclassics.yorku.ca/Stroop/

Ligon, E. M. A., Genetic study of color naming and word reading. *Amer. J. Psychol.*

Lund, F. H., The role of practice in speed of association. *J. Exper. Psychol.*

Telford, C. W., Differences in responses to colors and their names. *J. Genet. Psychol.*

Warner, B. R. Practice in associating color names with colors. *Psychol. Rev.*

APPENDICES

Appendix 1: Informed Consent

Dear participants, parents and legal guardians,

we are performing an experiment as part of our Internal Assessment for our IB Psychology class. We are investigating the interferences of serial verbal reactions. We would like to ask you to be part of our experiment.

If you agree to take part in this experiment, you should know that:

- All data that we obtain will be kept confidential and anonymous.
- You may stop participating in this experiment at any time.
- You shall receive information about the nature of the experiment and our results after we have obtained results.

The experiment will take about five minutes to complete.

If you agree, we ask that you sign the form below and to fill in the following information relevant to our experiment.

2. EXAMPLE TWO (22/22)

Name: 'An experiment to investigate the impact of levels of processing on the recall of a list of words

Author: Anonymous

Session: May 2022

Level: HL

Contents

Introduction 3
Exploration 5
Analysis 8
Evaluation 10
References 13
Appendices
        Appendix 1. (Informed Consent Form) 14
        Appendix 2. (Standardized Instructions) 15
        Appendix 3. (Numbered Answer Sheet) 16
        Appendix 4. (List of 40 adjectives) 17
        Appendix 5. (Google Form Response) 18
        Appendix 6. (Debriefing Notes) 18
        Appendix 7. (Procedure) 19
        Appendix 8. (Raw and Processed Data) 20
        Appendix 9. (Inferential Statistics) 21

Introduction

Memory is the complex cognitive process responsible for encoding, storing and retrieving information from the brain. **Craik and Lockhart (1972)** developed the **levels of processing theory** which states that recall from memory is dependent on the level at which information is processed and the deeper information is processed, the longer it will last in the memory and the easier it will be to recall (McLeod, 2007). The theory explains that information can be processed on a shallow level, through **structural processing** (encoding the physical appearance of something) as well as **phonemic processing** (encoding sound) or information can be processed deeply, through **semantic processing** (encoding the meaning of a word, relating it to similar things or linking it to previous knowledge). Craik and Lockhart argued that recall ability is independent of rehearsal and instead, information is transferred from **short term memory (STM)** to **long term memory (LTM)** based on the level at which it is processed. Deeper levels of processing, such as self-reference processing, results in the creation of **self-schemas** which transfers information from STM to LTM.

The study being replicated in the investigation was the **Rogers, Kuiper and Kirker (1977)** study of self-referential encoding. The aim of the study was to investigate the extent to which the self is implicated in processing personal information (Rogers, 1977). 59 undergraduate students were presented with adjectives in two experiments and were asked to complete one of four different tasks which forced different levels of processing: structural, phonemic, semantic or self-reference. The results demonstrated that the adjectives within the self-reference task were recalled the best in comparison to adjectives in the structural, phonemic or semantic processing conditions. This demonstrated that self-reference appeared to produce recall superior to any other task with different levels of processing. Rogers, Kuiper and Kirker concluded that as part of the human information-processing system, the self functions as a schema which is most deeply involved in processing and recall ability of information. Self-referencing was shown to be a form of deep processing. Tasks which utilize deep processing create strong traces in the memory which are later used as cues to assist recall. Since personal data is processed using schema-like structures, it is the most prominent in long-term memory. Therefore, when relating information to themselves, individuals are more likely to recall information than in any other level of processing.

The aim of our investigation was **to investigate the self-reference effect** and its impact on recall ability. Recall ability is especially important in school, so our research aimed to give students a better understanding of how accurate long-term memories can be formed most effectively. This would be especially useful in improving school performance through the development of more effective, self-referent memorization techniques to aid in recall, an important skill for all IB courses.

IV: There were two conditions of the independent variable, the structural processing condition (participants asked to answer whether the word had a letter "e" in it) and the self-reference processing condition (whether the word was a good descriptor of their personality).

DV: The dependent variable was the number of words from the list of 40 words which were correctly recalled.

Research hypothesis: The participants who are in the self-reference processing condition will recall more accurate words from the list of 40 words than those in the structural processing condition.

Null hypothesis: There will be no significant difference in the amount of accurate words recalled from a list of 40 words whether the participants are in the self-reference processing or structural processing condition.

Exploration

Research Design:

An **independent measures design** was used to carry out the research consisting of two separate conditions of the independent variable, structural processing and self-reference processing, with an equal number of participants randomly allocated into one of the two conditions. The random allocation was done based on two separate participant lists, one for boys and one for girls, of which every other girl and every other boy were assigned into the same condition while the remainder were assigned to the second condition. This was done in order to mitigate any individual differences while maintaining a balance between the two genders and the number of participants. The independent measures design was necessary in order to avoid the participants developing demand characteristics by learning the purpose of the study (as they would have already been asked to recall the words in the previous condition) and consequently trying to memorize the 40 words.

Sampling Technique:

The sampling technique used in this study was **opportunity sampling**: participants were chosen based on their availability and willingness to participate. As IB students given a week to conduct the IA research, we were limited by a time-constraint as well as wider face-to-face contact due to COVID-19, which meant that the most quick and easily convenient participants were used, other IB highschool students.

Sample characteristics:

Based on opportunity sampling, **20 IB highschool students** aged **16 to 17** were used to carry out the research. There was an even split between the gender of the total participants as well as between the gender in each condition of the independent variable (10 males, 10 females, 5 per group). Additionally, the sample did not include any current or previous IB psychology students as they would have been familiar with the study and its aim, causing them to change their natural behavior by actively memorizing the words. The sample included only 16 and 17 year old students in order to reduce any impact of age and make the results more comparable between the two conditions of the IV. It was also ensured that none of the participants had extreme visual or auditory impairment which would hinder their ability to participate in the research through inability to listen to instructions, see the projected words, or view the distraction task.

Controlled Variables:

Numerous extraneous variables were controlled. **Standardized instructions** were given to each group of participants with only the IV differing in the script, in order to avoid any difference in word choice impacting the results. The **equal number of males and females** in each condition ensured that gender imbalance would not impact the results even if one gender had a tendency to perform better. Each of the 40 words were shown to the participants for the same amount of time (10 seconds) in order to avoid any words being recalled due to rehearsal and transference to long term memory. The list of 40 words also contained an **equal number of adjectives with the letter "e" as without the letter "e"** (20 with and 20 without) so that participants in the structural processing condition would not recall words based on their distinctiveness. After showing the list of words, a one minute video was shown as a **distraction task** in order to eliminate recall of words due to the **recency effect**.

Materials:

The materials utilized were carefully chosen to maximize efficiency and limit confounding variables. Consent forms (appendix 1) were sent to all participants as a Google form which was a fast and contactless way to submit personal details and permission to participate given the ongoing COVID-19 pandemic. The 40 adjectives used to describe personality (appendix 4) were compiled from ESOL courses (Words that describe personality, n.d.) on a Google slides presentation and standardized instructions (appendix 2) were given on a Google Doc. A blank "answer form" Google Doc numbered 1-40 was created for each participant (appendix 3) which they accessed from their individual laptops. Two additional Google forms were created for participants to type the words they recalled, one for each condition, making the results easily distinguishable (appendix 5). An iPhone was used to time the 2 minute recall period, ensuring participants had equal amounts of time to write their responses. Finally, a debriefing script (appendix 6) was created to ensure that ethical considerations were met.

Procedure: See appendix 7

Analysis

Figure 1: Descriptive statistics table

Experimental Condition	Average number of words correctly recalled	Standard Deviation of words correctly recalled
Condition 1: Structural Processing	5.8	1.93
Condition 2: Self-reference Processing	10.1	4.43

Descriptive statistics:

In order to provide a better understanding of the results, two measures of central tendency and dispersion were applied: mean and standard deviation. The mean was calculated to find the average number of words correctly recalled in each group while the standard deviation was used to calculate how much an average participant varied from the mean.

Based on the calculation of the mean, a clear difference can be seen between the average number of correct words recalled within the structural and self-reference processing conditions. On average, 5.8 words were recalled by the structural processing condition while the self-reference processing condition had a significantly higher mean of 10.1 words correctly recalled, demonstrating an overall tendency to recall more words correctly when relating the words to oneself, thereby showing self-referencing. The data also clearly shows that the standard deviation in the structural processing condition was 1.93 and it was 4.43 for the self-reference processing condition, demonstrating a greater variance and spread of results in the deeper processing condition. The difference in standard deviation between the two conditions could be due to extraneous variables such as participants not understanding certain words or occasionally conversing despite being instructed against doing so.

Figure 2: Descriptive statistics graph

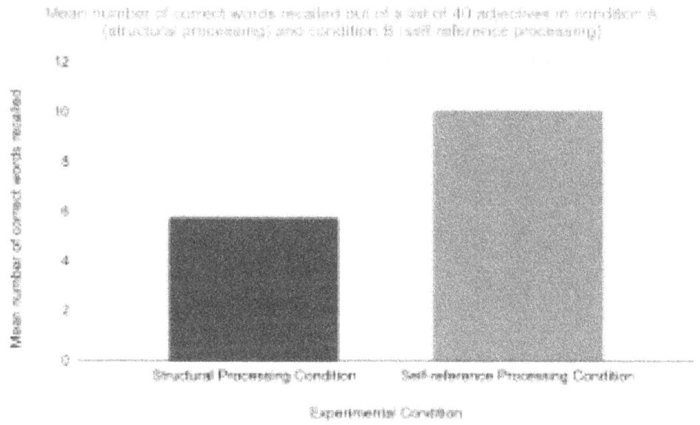

Mean number of correct words recalled out of a list of 40 adjectives in condition A (structural processing) and condition B (self-reference processing)

Inferential statistics

The **Mann-Whitney U** test was selected to calculate the inferential statistics since the experiment utilized an independent measures design, there was a small sample size and lack of standard distribution of data was reduced to ordinal. Based on the test, the value of U A = **82.5** exceeds the critical value of 73 at $p \leq 0.05$. Therefore, it appears that our results are **significant** so we can reject the null hypothesis and accept the research hypothesis that participants who are in the self-reference processing condition are able recall more words from a list of 40 words accurately than those in the structural processing condition.

Evaluation

The results of the experiment are similar to the results obtained by Rogers, Kuiper and Kirker in reference to the pattern of increased recall ability in the deeper processing condition, self-reference processing, in comparison to the structural processing condition. Both experiments provided evidence for the superior incidental recall of adjectives in a self-reference processing experimental condition, demonstrating the impact of self-involvement in memory retrieval. The findings of the research are directly in line with the levels of processing theory proposed by Craick and Lockhart as manipulating the independent variable showed a significant change in the mean number of words correctly recalled, indicating enhanced memory through deeper processing such as self-referencing. As the participants were asked to answer whether the word was an accurate descriptor of their personality (self-reference processing) in both the original study as well as our recreation of the study, the words were more likely to be transferred to long term memory to be used later for recall in comparison to shallower processing methods.

A **strength** of the independent measures **design** was that participants completed the experiment without knowing the aim, due to the misleading answer sheet which led participants to believe their only task was to answer yes or no questions, thereby reducing the chance of developing demand characteristics. However, a **limitation** of the independent measures design is the risk of contamination between the two conditions. As there were two different groups of participants, those in the first group could have discussed the aim and details of the study with participants in the second experimental condition. A **modification** to avoid any chances of contamination would be to conduct the experiment with each experimental condition directly after each other. As the participants in the first condition leave the room, those in the second condition should enter immediately to prevent discussion about the study between groups.

One of the biggest **strengths** of the experimental **procedure** was the inclusion of the one minute video as a distraction task after the participants were shown the list of 40 words. The distraction task was controlling for the recency effect, ensuring that the participants did not recall any words simply because they appeared at the end of the list, making them the most recently processed. A **limitation** of the procedure was caused by conducting the experiment in groups as students occasionally talked amongst themselves despite being instructed not to. A **modification** to overcome this issue would be to conduct the experiment on participants one at a time which would limit any distractions to the task, ensuring participants' full attention to the experiment.

The **strength** of the **sample** of 16-17 year old male and female IB students was that both genders were equally involved and equally distributed into the two conditions, 5 males and 5 females in the structural processing condition and 5 males and 5 females in the self-reference processing condition. Controlling for gender ensured the elimination of any gender differences which could make either male or female participants perform better in the tasks. Using non-psychology students also meant that the participants were unfamiliar with the study and its aim which allowed minimization of demand characteristics. The sample was somewhat **limited** as the reading levels and language proficiency of participants was not measured. This could impact the ability of participants to read the words and answer quickly enough, giving less time for the processing to occur for those who are less proficient in English reading. A **modification** for this would be to conduct the research with only proficient, native English speakers as their performance would not be hindered by limited reading capabilities.

From the study it can be concluded that self-reference processing (deep level) results in enhanced recall ability of words in comparison to structural processing (shallow level) in 16 and 17 year old IB highschool students.

BIBLIOGRAPHY + APPENDICES OMITTED

3. EXAMPLE THREE (19/22)

Name: How do leading questions affect eyewitness testimonies?

Author: Anonymous

Session: May 2022

Level: HL

Table of Contents

Internal Assessment 1

Introduction 3

Exploration 4

    Design 4

    Participants and ethics 5

    Materials 6

    Procedure 6

Analysis 7

    Description 7

    Statistical significance 8

Evaluation 9

    Links to the theory 9

    Design 9

    Sample 10

    Procedure and modifications 10

    Conclusion 11

References 12

Appendices 13

        Appendix 1- briefing 13

        Appendix 2- debriefing 13

        Appendix 3- letter of consent 13

        Appendix 4- raw data 14

        Appendix 5- calculated figures 15

        Appendix 6- materials 15

        Appendix 7- statistical significance (u-test) 15

Introduction

The cognitive approach focuses on various thinking processes and human memory. In the past, cognitive researchers have investigated how knowledge is stored, retrieved and its reliability. According to the schema theory, schemas are mental representations developed from prior knowledge and experience, which help us interpret vast amounts of information, predicting situational outcomes based on what has happened before. The misinformation effect refers to the common interference between post-event information and the actual memory of the original event, which is closely connected to reconstructive memory theory (RMT). RMT states that we must consciously rebuild our memories every time we try to remember something.

All this is significant when eyewitness testimonies are used in criminal trials since the flawlessness of human memory is relied upon heavily. In the past decades, the perfection of memory has been disputed and most experts agree that the process of rebuilding our memories is influenced by our beliefs, feelings, or unrelated memories. Additionally, only fragmented memory traces of past events are stored in our memory, rather than a complete record. Hence, in the memory recollection process, the incomplete record causes us to make mistakes and fill in the gaps in our memory with incorrect information. This is where schemas play a role since information consistent with our schemas will be remembered well and the rest will be distorted or forgotten.

This outlines the problem with the presence of leading questions in eyewitness testimonies, which was the focus of the Loftus and Palmer 1974 (LP) study. That study aimed to "test the hypothesis that the language used in eyewitness testimonies can alter memory".[1]

---

[1] Loftus and Palmer | Simply Psychology

The results have shown that the estimated speed was the highest in the 'smashed' condition at 40.8 mph and lowest in the 'contacted' group at 31.8 mph. Stating that memories can be influenced by framing questions and supporting the idea of reconstructive memory.

This study aims to determine whether the verb intensity in investigatory questions influences an eye-witness's memory of a car accident. Thus, it is a partial replicate of the LP study. The leading question, regarding a car accident, will contain verbs with different intensities, which is the independent variable (IV). Whereas the dependent variable (DV) is the average speed estimate, measured by taking the average of the participants' estimations. This topic is worth studying because it helps determine the reliability of memory, impacting not only everyday scenarios but also court proceedings and other professional situations.

H_0: The difference in verb intensities utilized in the leading question will not have a statistically significant effect on the average speed estimates of the 20 participants.

H_1: The participants' average speed estimate will be significantly higher when the intensity of the verb "smashed" utilized in the leading question is greater than the less intense verb "contacted".

Exploration

Design

This experiment utilizes an independent measures design, preventing participants from discovering the aim of the experiment. This method eliminates the order effect and ensures that the final results are not unnecessarily distorted. It was not possible to control individual participant variables, but the larger sample size negates this factor to a certain extent. The controls in this experiment are the device utilized for video projection, the controlled school environment, the participants' unawareness regarding the aim of the experiment, time of day and the age of the participants. The experiment was conducted in a consistent classroom environment to avoid distractions, between 11 am and 2 pm. All participants were of a similar age, and they all watched the same 9-second video, a replication of the LP study crash footage[2], for increased consistency. The IV in this study is the verb intensity in the leading question since it is being purposefully changed. Whereas the DV is the average speed estimate. Simply, the difference between the participants' average speed estimates will either prove or disprove the influence of leading questions on memory recollection.

Participants and ethics

The convenience sampling method was utilized, because securing a sample from the section of a population that is most readily available, is a simple and most time-effective solution. Selected participants consisted of 20 multilingual students from an international school, aged 16-18 years old. International Baccalaureate students were chosen, because of their presumably increased enthusiasm for psychological research. The main confounding variables were participants' driving experience and the state of mind at the time of the experiment, affecting effort or motivation levels. Sharing of information with the participants was done on a need-to-know basis, limiting their knowledge about the aim of the experiment. Participants were randomly allocated to one of the two conditions, and they consented[3] to be a part of the study, maintaining ethical standards. Afterwards, appropriate debriefing was

---

[2] Loftus and Palmer Replication Crash Footage - YouTube
[3] Appendix 3 - letter of consent

conducted to provide participants with a full explanation of the study hypothesis, the reason for the deceit and to receive feedback.

Materials

See Appendix 6.[4]

Procedure

The testing procedure itself began by taking group one, 10 participants, into a predetermined controlled environment, with video projecting capabilities (classroom). The same procedure applied to group number two, but the experiment was carried out at the same time on a different day. Participants were seated with an adequate view of the video projection and received the briefing.[5] They were all simultaneously shown the car crash video and each participant was handed a paper with a single question about estimating the speed of the vehicles in a car crash. The exact wording of the question was, *"About how fast were the cars going when they smashed into each other?"*. However, one group had a question containing the verb, "smashed", whereas the other group had the word, "contacted". The answers were collected for further analysis. The participants received a thorough debriefing[6] and were subsequently dismissed since the experimental part of the study was concluded. During the entire experiment, there was no communication between the individual participants.

---

[4] Appendix 6- materials
[5] Appendix 1- briefing
[6] Appendix 2- debriefing

Analysis

	Calculated figures					
Verb	Mean speed estimate (km/h)	Median	Mode	Standard deviation	Mann Whitney (u-test)	Statistical Significance (t-test)
"Smashed"	63.6	64.5	65	11.69	p=0.0559	p=0.0826
"Contacted"	54.5	55	50	10.39		

Figure 1: Statistical Significance

Description

Preliminarily, the data[7] collected from the two groups of 10 participants suggests that the leading verbs utilized had an impact on the average speed estimates of the participants. The mean estimate *(Figure 1)* in the more intense "smashed" condition, was 63.6 km/h. Whilst the mean estimate in the less intense "contacted" group was 54.5 km/h. Hence, the difference of 9.1 km/h between the two conditions appears to support the alternative hypothesis. This is further supported by the medians[8] and modes[9] of each data set. The difference between the individual modes is 15 km/h and the difference between the medians is 9.5 km/h.

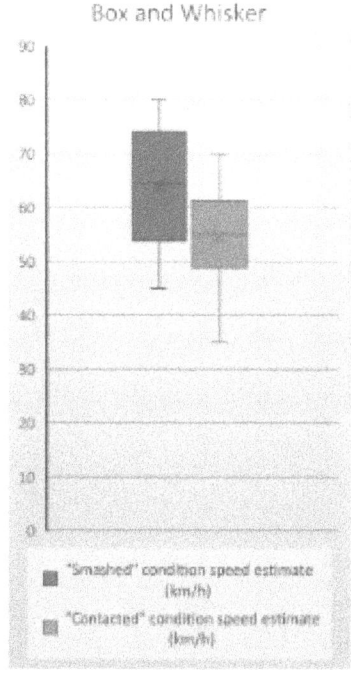

Figure 2: Box and Whisker

In the entire data set, there are no outliers. The value furthest from the rest is highlighted in Appendix 4[10], but it is not a significant outlier. Standard deviations[11] are very similar in both conditions, the difference is just 1.3 km/h. Meaning that the distribution of values from the mean is similar in both data sets, with the "smashed" condition being slightly greater. The results are similarly slightly negatively skewed. The data

---

[7] Appendix 4- raw data
[8] Appendix 5- calculated figures
[9] Appendix 5- calculated figures
[10] Appendix 5- calculated figures
[11] Appendix 5- calculated figures

points certainly overlap, meaning that some individuals from the "contacted" group had a higher speed estimate than certain participants from the "smashed" group. This may have been caused by personal participant variables or by the fact that humans are unable to reliably estimate vehicle speed. Nevertheless, this overlap does not appear to be significant, and the mean values still imply a significant disparity between the two conditions.

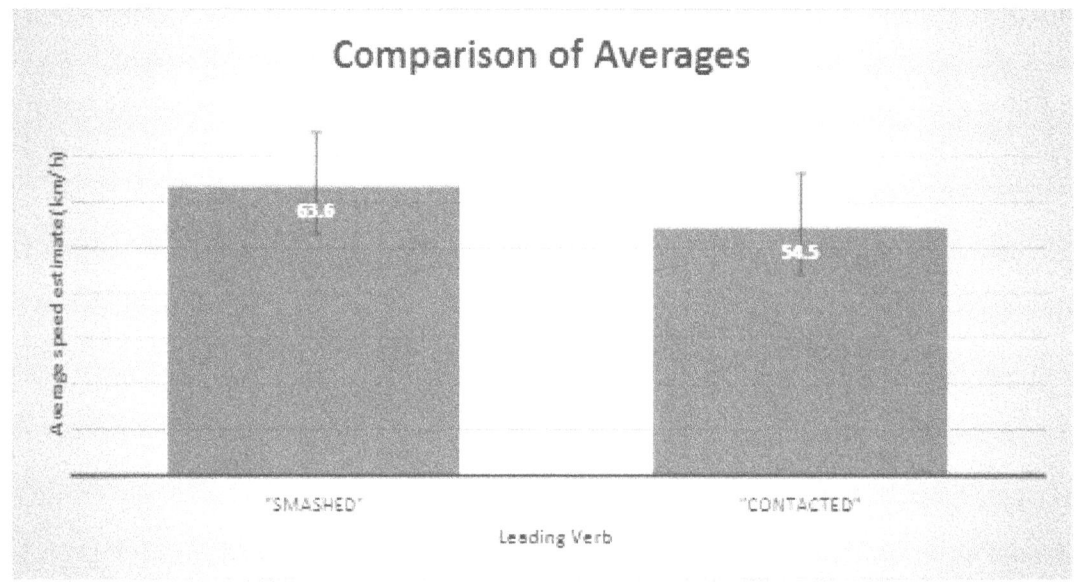

Figure 3: Comparison of Averages

Statistical significance

To assess the statistical significance of these results, t-test and Mann Whitney (u-test) were performed. These tests were deemed appropriate, mainly because the t-test determines whether there is a significant difference between the means of two groups and the u-test compares whether there is a difference in the DV for two independent groups. Perfectly suitable for this independent samples study, producing p-values. In statistics, the p-value measures the probability that an observed difference could have occurred just by random chance. If the p-value is p≤0.05, the results are considered statistically significant. However, if p>0.05, the results are not statistically significant, and the null hypothesis must be maintained.

The statistical significance[12] of this study's results according to the t-test is 0.0826 and according to the u-test 0.0559. Hence the results are not considered statistically significant, the difference between the mean estimates was not sufficient and the null hypothesis must be maintained. Simply, purely based on the results of this study, it is not possible to conclude that different verb intensities utilized in the leading questions influence speed estimation in humans.

Evaluation

Links to the theory

These findings appear to support schema theory and reconstructive memory since the verb intensities in the leading questions did have some effect on the mean speed estimations. However, since there was no statistical significance to these results, this study cannot be solely used to support the aforementioned theories. Nevertheless, the results from the original LP study were statistically significant. Hence the results of this study may be explained by multiple factors. There was a sampling bias present in this study since all participants were students, who perhaps did not have the schema related to this particular scenario, due to their young age and lack of driving experience. Or participants may have lacked motivation and not taken the estimations seriously enough. Both factors might have influenced the findings and resulted in a difference from the original study.

Design

The independent measures design was appropriate because it generally ensures increased external validity since more participants are utilized. However, the negative is that

---

[12] Appendix 7- statistical significance (u-test)

individual participant differences can often lead to discrepancies, causing false conclusions. In this study, the individual participants could have had different schemas and varied levels of car-related knowledge. Moreover, their motivation and effort levels were also different, negatively impacting results, increasing standard deviation, and causing statistical insignificance. The increased number of participants was not sufficient to counteract these negative impacts.

Sample

The convenience sampling method employed allowed for a cheap, simple, and efficient execution. Fortunately, the proportion between male and female participants was also maintained. All participants were selected from a consistent environment, they were of a similar age and intellectual development, helping the validity of the findings. However, this sampling method, unfortunately, limited the ability to generalize findings to the overall population, because of the different reasons why some people chose to participate, and others did not. Additionally, individual participant variables (effort, motivation, car-related knowledge) were not controlled, since it would be difficult to do objectively, damaging result validity.

Procedure and modifications

One strength of our procedure was only utilising the most and least intense verbs from the original study, simplifying the testing process and producing more distinct results. Another strength of the procedure was the fact that both groups were tested in the exact same classroom, and they were seated identically. Moreover, all participants received the exact same briefing and debriefing, limiting unnecessary confounding variables. One limitation that we identified when testing the first group was that we did not specify the speed estimation units ahead of the experiment or in the briefing. We quickly rectified this error and eliminated this mistake when testing the second group. However, the first group was already affected. In hindsight, we should have thought of this before testing and clearly state the speed estimation units. This confounding variable could have been eliminated. Lastly, another limitation related to the leading question was realized when testing the first group. Some participants were not sure which car's speed they should estimate since in the video a total of 3 cars were shown. We originally thought that it was obvious since only one car was in focus. Nevertheless, this misunderstanding could have been prevented by stating the colour of the main car in the briefing.

Conclusion

In conclusion, from our study, we are not able to conclude that leading questions influence eyewitness testimonies, due to the statistical insignificance of our results. Thus, we must maintain the null hypothesis. This could perhaps be rectified by increasing the sample size and including more verbs,to better match the original study.

BIBLIOGRAPHY + APPENDICES OMITTED

4. EXAMPLE FOUR (21/22)

Name: Inducing System 2 Thinking Through Metacognitive Challenges

Author: Anonymous

Session: May 2021

Level: HL

I. INTRODUCTION:

William James is considered to be one of the leading psychologists and philosophers of the 19th century, well-known for his work in establishing psychology as a field of study and his multiple theories that have aided to its development and knowledge in this current era. One theory in which he created the foundations for is the two-system theory. James suggested that humans when processing information use two kinds of thinking; associative and true reasoning. Whilst what he associated with the thinking processes is no longer believed in-- associative thinking is reproductive from past experiences and true reasoning is productive as it can understand and work with new information-- the concept of the two systems of thinking still stands today (Sloman 1996). In 2003, Daniel Kahneman interpreted this theory, suggesting the intuitive and rational thinking systems. Intuitive thinking, also known as System 1, is considered to be the automatic, instinctive and emotionally driven process and rational thinking, System 2, is the slower, effortful and deliberate process. It has been shown that system 1 is the default process, reflecting the idea that human beings are cognitive misers, aiming to solve problems as simply and efficiently as possible, instead of being more reflective of the decisions made (Kahneman 2003).

Alter et al. (2007) further studied and expanded the research of both William James and Kahneman (2003) in their own study, wherein they aimed to see if it was possible to deliberately make a person switch from system 1 to system 2. Alter et al. (2007) had 40 undergraduate students take a cognitive reflective test (CRT), which was either printed in an easy to read font or a hard to read font, making this their independent variable. The findings revealed that the students who experienced disfluency, the hard to read font, answered more of the CRT questions correctly than the fluency group.

These results could be explained by the two-system theory; by exposing the participants to metacognitive challenges, they were forced into using rational thinking. Rational thinking requires the participants to take more time when thinking of the question, leading to a higher chance of a correct answer. The results proved that system 2 was being used and not system 1, thus supporting the two-system theory.

The aim of this study is to determine whether it is possible to purposefully shift between system 1 and system 2 thinking, by exposing participants to metacognitive challenges such as type of font. This investigation is interesting to look into, as it can show that one can deliberately switch to rational thinking by simply making a situation disfluent, forcing them to take longer to process it. The findings of this study can be used to one's advantage to increase both their understanding and performance in learning.

The null hypothesis states that there will be no significant difference in performance on the Cognitive Reflective Test, based on a score out of five, between being given a fluent or disfluent text.

The research hypothesis is that the participants given the questions in a disfluent font (Homemade Apples, 9pt, dark grey 1) will use rational thinking and thus perform better on the Cognitive Reflective Test (number of questions, out of five, answered correctly) than the participants with questions in an easy to read font (Times New Roman, 12pt, black).

II. EXPLORATION:

Each participant took part in this experiment once, hence making it an independent measures design. Due to how different the two conditions of the independent variable are, the participants might be able to understand the aim of the experiment if they were to be exposed to both conditions, which could lead to demand characteristics. Additionally, the participants would have practice with the nature of the questions given, allowing them to perform better the second time.

A convenience sample technique was employed. This technique involves selecting participants from their availability and convenience. Due to performing this experiment at school during the day, only certain classes, and so participants, were available to us whilst we were free. We did, however, make sure that the classes chosen were IB English A classes, as that was a control needed for this investigation.

The sample consisted of 44 IB English A students, half of which were 12th-grade students and the other half 11th-grade students. It was believed that all of these participants would provide the highest levels of English language proficiency, adding to the control of the experiment. This sample was chosen as high and standardised levels of English understanding are important in order to understand exactly what the questions are asking, without any confusion of the language used in the question. By narrowing language levels and finding similarities within the students, it limits the amount of the confounding variables that could interfere with the results. Additionally, participants were aged between 16 and 18 years old. This age group was chosen, additionally to taking IB classes, as they are thought to have high levels of maturity that will answer the questions appropriately.

The Cognitive Reflection Test is a questionnaire that is designed to challenge a person's inclination to answer a question based on instinctive reaction and instead answer it with a reflective thought process. The CRT used in this study consisted of five questions (appendix i), three from the original test (Frederick, p.27) and two additional 'riddle' questions (*Fun Logic*, n.d. and *Word Problems*, n.d.). The two extra questions were added as means of control, as they are considered easier than the three other questions and will show the participant's basic knowledge of reflective questions.

Each year level was allocated to both conditions. This was done so that the age of the participants could be controlled and limit its potential influence on their performance. In both conditions, the researchers read from a standardised briefing statement (appendix ii) when giving instructions, as a way to limit any researcher expectancies. Participants were asked to sign consent forms (appendix iii). The CRT was distributed to each participant, placed face down on the desk. When told so, participants were allowed to turn over their tests and begin. A 10-minute time limit was set. When finished, participants occupied themselves quietly whilst their peers completed the test, until the time was over. Researchers collected the papers and debriefed the participants (appendix iv).

III. ANALYSIS:

Table 1: Descriptive Statistics (appendix v)

	Fluent Condition	Disfluent Condition
Mean	3.54	2.68
Standard Deviation	1.34	1.17

These results, as measured by the participants' score on the CRT, showed that it was ratio data, so the mean and standard deviation of the data was calculated, as they are the appropriate measurements for this data. The results (Table 1) show that the disfluent condition answered less questions correctly (M = 2.68) than the fluent condition (M = 3.54). Additionally, the disfluent group had a lower standard deviation (SD = 1.17) than the other condition (SD = 1.34), meaning that the values from the fluent group are spread out, resulting in a wide range of values. Despite the wide range, there are no outliers or values that have been excluded from the data.

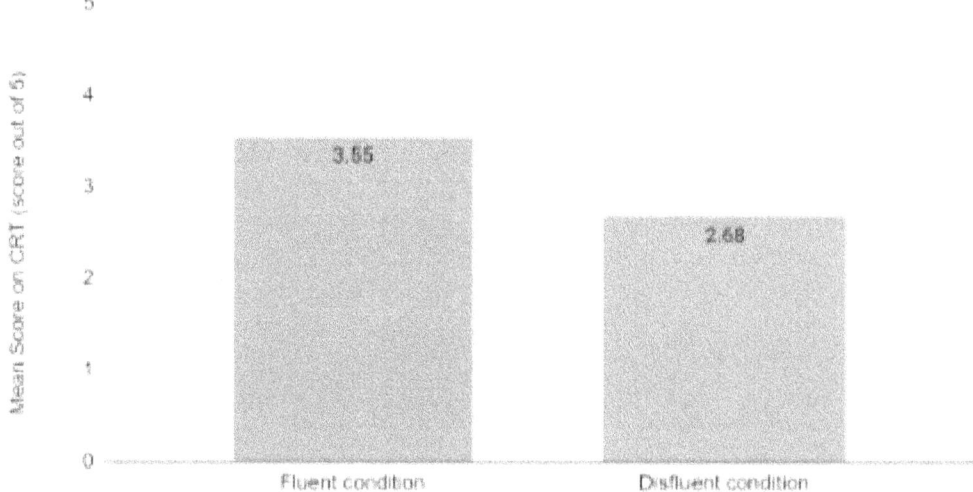

Figure. 1: The Effect of Fluency of a Text on the Mean Score on a CRT

Despite the results coming to the opposite conclusion of the research hypothesis, an inferential test must be performed in order to determine whether the null hypothesis must be accepted or rejected. In order to find inferential statistics for this independent measure investigation and ratio data, an unrelated t-test was performed (appendix vi). A t-test shows whether there is a significant difference between the means of the two conditions, determining if those results could have happened by chance. This can be determined by the p-value, which is found when performing the t-test. P-values are measured by a decimal which shows the probability of the results not occurring by chance. The accepted value range is less than 0.05. The p-value, in this investigation, is 0.013841. This result is lower than the accepted value meaning that there is a statistical significance, thus resulting in a rejection of the null hypothesis. Usually, by rejecting the null hypothesis, there would be an automatic acceptance of the research hypothesis. However, the results derived from this experiment lead to an opposite conclusion than what the research hypothesis suggests; the fluent condition answered more questions correctly on the test, hence performing better than the disfluent condition. The result of the t-test suggests that the fluency of the font used in writing the questions has a significant effect on one's performance on the test, however, for a reason other than the expected theory.

IV. EVALUATION:

The theory of this investigation is the two-system theory. The theory states that when using system 2, cognitive performance is greater than when using system 1. The researchers of the original study, Alter et al. (2007), discovered that it was possible to deliberately switch between the two systems by exposing the participants to a cognitive challenge, such as a disfluent text. This would stimulate rational thinking, thus moving the participants from system 1 to system 2 thinking, which was proven by participants with the disfluent text performing better on the CRT than the participants with the fluent text. However, our results of this investigation do not support those findings. We got the opposite results, showing that the fluent condition had an overall greater mean result than the disfluent group. One explanation for this might be that due to the school and test settings, all of the participants might already be using system 2 thinking, therefore using rational thinking. By not exposing the fluent condition to any difficulty, it allows those participants to continue performing at a high level. The disfluent condition, however, was exposed to a challenging font, which, in theory, would have resulted in higher performance. However, instead of challenging the participants into thinking through the questions more thoroughly, the complicated font given might have frustrated them instead, causing them to skim over the question and not reflect on it much. This would cause them to switch back into system 1 thinking, hence causing them to perform poorly.

A strength is that it was an independent measure design. By using this design, the participants were not able to determine the aim and it removes the possibility of order effects that could have potentially affected the results.

Another strength that can be identified is our sample, as there was an equal number of 12th to 11th graders in the overall study and distributed within both conditions. This controlled for the possible confounding variable of age and so, matured cognitive abilities.

A strength in our procedure is the standardised test that all participants took. The test consisted of the same questions that were in the same order every time. This meant that the dependent variable was operationalised and simple to measure.

A limitation in the design is the independent measure. Whilst the strengths do outweigh the limitations, it does not completely eradicate the possible negative effects it can have on the results. It is unknown whether the participants answered the questions correctly due to the font and the use of system 2 or if it was simply based on their cognitive abilities. All the participants have a variety of different cognitive abilities, some more able to answer these questions than others. This factor was not measured, so the researchers have no prior knowledge of the individuals' cognitive ability. This leads to the uncertainty of the results. A modification that could be applied is to perform more prior research on the participants. Asking their mathematics class, their academic orientation (maths, language, or art-based) could provide information on their baseline cognitive abilities.

A limitation with the convenience sampling technique and the student sample is that the participants, due to the setting of the experiment, might have already been using system 2 thinking. As mentioned in the discussion, this might have caused inaccurate results, apropos to the original study. The modification for this limitation can be taken from the original experiment, wherein the participants consisted of student volunteers who were not currently in a class. This ensured that they were not in a working environment and were most likely not already using system 2 thinking. This method of sampling could be used in a modified version of this particular experiment.

Additionally, there is a limitation in the student sample, such as participant variability and demand characteristics, such as language. Although we tried to control English language proficiency, by using participants who take English A classes, there was still a lot of variety, due to the experiment taking place at an international school. It was seen that there were more non-native English speakers than native English speakers. Furthermore, the non-native speakers have all been speaking English for a number of different years, thus further differentiating the group. This meant that we were unable to control for their understanding of the question, therefore, influencing the results.

A procedural limitation is the font used. We thought that by giving the participants a highly challenging font, it would compel the participants to use system 2. As aforementioned in the discussion, the font was perhaps too challenging. A modification is to make the disfluent text less challenging, perhaps simply changing the colour, size and italicising it. This would still require the participants to read slower than usual, resulting in them using rational thinking, but without putting them through too much difficulty in simply understanding the font.

BIBLIOGRAPHY + APPENDICES OMITTED

5. EXAMPLE FIVE (21/22)

Name The effect of a 30 second delay on the recall of the last 5 words (recency effect)

Author: Anonymous

Session: May 2022

Level: HL

Table of contents

Introduction	2
Exploration	4
Analysis	8
Evaluation	11
Bibliography	13
Appendices	14
Appendix A	14
Appendix B	16
Appendix C	18
Appendix D	20
Appendix E	21
Appendix F	23
Appendix G	25

Introduction

Memory in humans works in complicated manners and many theories and models exist to explain the working of memory. The multi-store model of memory - proposed by Richard Atkinson and Richard Shiffrin is a structural model which assumes 3 unitary stores of memory; a sensory register, STM (short term memory) & LTM (long term memory). Atkinson and Shiffrin in 1968 Each of the memory stores encodes memory in separate manners. The capacity and the duration of the memory in each of the memory stores is different. The sensory organs sense the information from the environment and this information then enters the sensory register. The sensory register stores sensory inputs as 'impressions'. If these impressions are given attention, they enter the STM. Here upto 7-9 chunks of information are stored for around 15 seconds. Upon continued rehearsal of the information in the STM will then be stored in the LTM. The LTM has indefinite capacity and duration of memory. The memories of the LTM are semantically encoded though can be visual/auditory. Miller's magic number - 7(plus or minus 2 items) suggests how the average adult can only store 5 - 9 chunks of information in their short-term memory. Though the short term memory does not talk about the size of each such chunk. The digit span test has also been used to show the size of short-term memory. The span of short-term memory is around 15-30 seconds though information can be recalled via verbal rehearsal or acoustic encoding. The information described in MSM passes through a linear way where there is an input, processing is conducted and then there is an output. While, the long term memory is rehearsed With the use of elaborative rehearsal. (Demir, 2021)

The presence of a multi store model of memory can also be seen via the serial position effect. The serial position effect was first discovered by the psychologist Hermann Ebbinghaus. The serial position effect is one's tendency to recall information depending upon the chronology of observing that information. The serial position effect describes the tendency to recall information at the end of the list better, known as the recency effect. The study being replicated for this experiment is Glanzer and Cunitz in 1966 about the recency effect. This study aimed to investigate STM as a store of memory and to investigate the recency effect in correlation with position of the information presented. The original study used a repeated measures design, the participants were presented with a 15 word list. The participants were asked to later recall the presented words. The participants were divided into 3 conditions, 2 being delayed recall where the participants were presented with a 'distraction task' And the other condition being immediate recall where the participants were immediately requested to begin writing the words they remembered from the list. In the study conducted by Glanzer and Cunitz, delaying the recall by 30 seconds and inducing a procedure preventing rehearsal led to the complete neutralization of the recency effect. And in the case of immediate recall the recency effect took place with much higher and accurate recall of the last few words. (Koppenaal & Glanzer, 1990)

Our investigation aims to examine whether an increase in time between presentation and recall will negatively affect the recency effect. This investigation will also have implications for students, as it uses samples of that age group. Allowing for better memorization techniques and suggesting better teaching strategies for such said students.

The **independent variable** in this study is the presence or absence of a 30-second delay between presentation and recall of a list of words. The **dependent variable** is the recency effect - the recall of the last 5 words from a list of 15 monosyllabic words.

Null hypothesis: The 30 second delay between presentation and recall of a list of words will have no effect on the recall of the last 5 words on the list shown (recency effect).

Research hypothesis: The 30 second delay between presentation and recall of a list of words will lead to significantly lowered recall of the last 5 words from the displayed list (recency effect).

Exploration

This exploration followed a laboratory experiment. In terms of design, an Independent Measures design was used. This design was used because we did not want participants to know the aim of the experiment and thus prevent demand characteristics. We also controlled for possible order effects such as practice effects.

The conducted experiment used opportunity sampling to procure the participant pool. Primarily so because the relevant audience which is students were already available in the school where the experiment was conducted. We were also limited in choice due to the ongoing pandemic. We selected a total of 30 participants, 15 in each condition. All the participants were IBDP students between the ages of 16-18. They were highly proficient fluent speakers of English. None of the participants were IBDP psychology students. The group of participants was rather diverse representing many racial and cultural backgrounds.

Many variables had to be controlled, to do so standardized instructions were used. The list of the words presented were standardized - all participants were presented the same monosyllabic list with 3 letters to keep the 'complexity' of the words the same all across. A random generator was used to produce these words. To avoid demand characteristics participants were experimented one at a time. All participants were brought to the same room to control environmental factors. The participants were also particularly requested to avoid writing any personal information such as their name on the paper provided in order to control any form of researcher bias. None of the participants were psychology students to prevent the expectancy effect from happening. To avoid familiarity with the study being referred to and thus demand characteristics. Finally, a distraction task that required participants to count backwards in three's from 360 for 30 seconds was used to prevent them from rehearsing the words during the 30 second delay.

For this experiment a computer to present the video containing the list of 15 words, an empty school classroom and a printed standardized consent form was used. The consent form was used to maintain ethical considerations, the consent form informed the participants of their ability to withdraw from the experiment at any time and information about the anonymity and confidentiality of their data. The empty classroom was used to maintain a stagnant-controlled environment in order to reduce external confounding stimulation from the environment. The computer was used to present the list of 15 words, similar to that of the original study by Glanzer and Cunitz.

All the participants were provided with a consent form (Appendix-A) which had to be signed in order to proceed with the study. The participants were reminded of their right to leave the experiment at any point in time and their right to withdraw any of their data from the study entirely. The participants were sent a debriefing mail (Appendix-D) explaining the study and its aim post experiment. Though, the participants were initially deceived as the aim of the study was not revealed.

The study baegan by random and even allocation of participants into 2 conditions - No Delay condition (Immediate free recall) & Delay condition (Delayed free recall - 30 seconds) . The participants were escorted to an empty room where - after the participants read and signed the consent form, the researcher read, out loud, the standardized instructions of the experiment to the participants (Appendix-B). Then, a 47 second video (Appendix-C) containing the 15 words was presented. A word was flashed for 1 second with a 2 second delay between each word. In the delay condition the participants were asked by the researcher to count back in 3's from 360 for 30 seconds as a distraction task in order to prevent rehearsal of the words from the displayed list. The participants then recalled the words onto an empty A4 sheet. The participants were given 3 minutes to complete this task. The participants in the immediate recall condition were directly requested to write down the initially presented words without a distraction task. Finally a debriefing email was sent to all participants.

Analysis

As our data generalizes the average percentage for each word in the last 5 word section of the list this is an inferential data set. Standard deviation is used to describe the central tendency of the data set as the serial position of the recalled words matters and because the recall decreases significantly in the delay condition, deeming mode or median as worse methods of calculating central tendency.

	Delay condition	No Delay condition
Mean percentage of correct recalls	45.26%	68%
Standard deviation	1.30	1.24

The table above depicts the mean percentage of correct recalls and the standard deviation of the words recalled in the two conditions.

The percentage of correct responses is higher in the no-delay condition (68%) as compared to the delay condition (45.26%) suggesting that the recency effect could have come into account. The standard deviation in the delay condition (1.3) is also higher than that of no-delay (1.24) suggesting that the data in the no-delay condition is less 'spread-out'.

To check for the presence of the recency effect the serial position effect can be graphed. This leads to what replicates the serial position curve which was initially produced in the results of the study Glanzer and Cunitz (1966). The curve was produced using the data from the "no-delay" condition (Appendix-G). The rise in the probability toward the end suggests the presence of the recency effect.

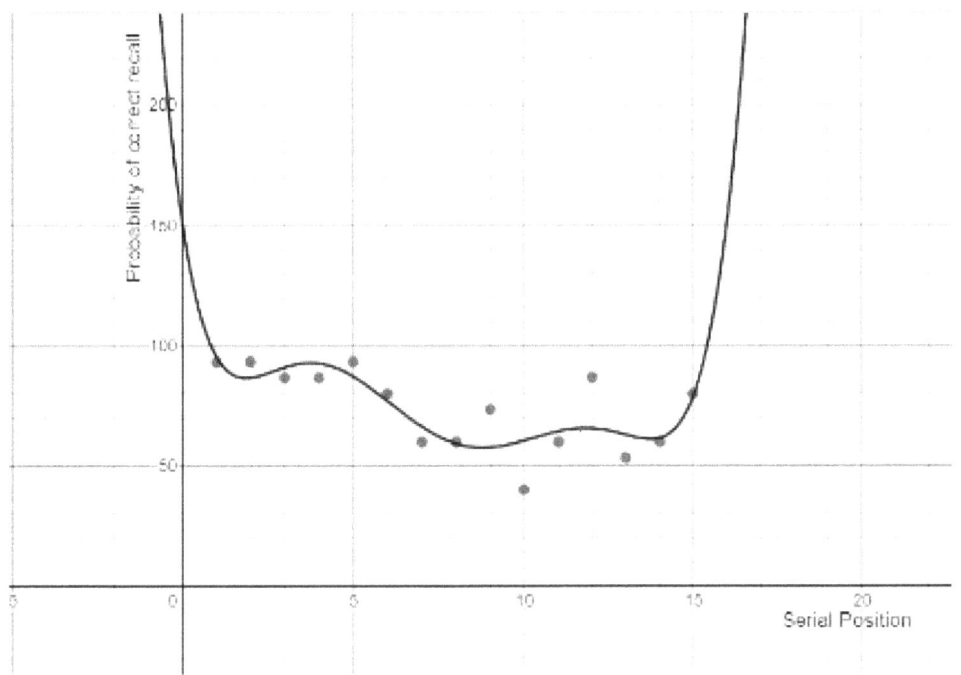

Fig - 1.2 Serial Position Curve (Produced via *"Desmos"*)

The percentage of the recall of the last 5 words of the list in both the conditions is presented below for comparison.

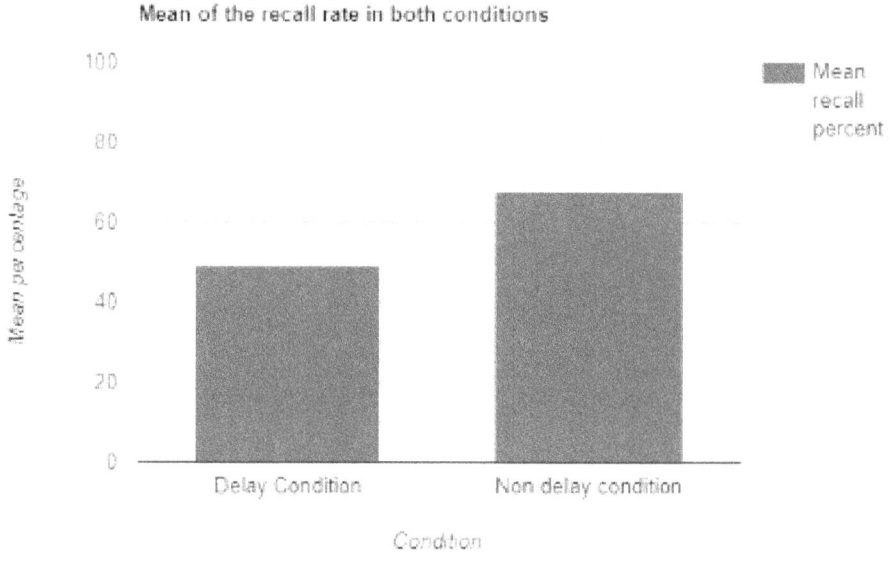

Fig 1.2 - Bar Graph (Produced with *"Bar Graph Maker"*)

Then, the Mann Whitney U test was conducted (*Social Science Statistics*) to check the significance of the data produced. (Appendix-E) As the data from this experiment was ordinal and not normally distributed the Mann whitney test was used instead of the Independent-t test. The U-value obtained from the test was 3 whereas the critical value of U at P <0.5 is 4 meaning the result is significant at p <0.5. So, the null hypothesis can successfully be rejected suggesting that: The 30 second delay between presentation and recall of a list of words will lead to significantly lowered recall of the last 5 words from the displayed list (recency effect) as compared to the no delay condition.

Evaluation

From the results it can be seen that a 30 second delay had an negative effect on the recency effect - a lower recall of the last 5 words. This can be supported by the Multi Store Model. This was because the increase in delay prevented the transfer of the last few words in the list from STM to LTM. The distraction task controlled for any possible rehearsal. This clearly shows that when there is an increased delay and rehearsal is prevented recency effect will be affected or the words at the end of a list will not be recalled.

The design of the experiment followed an independent measures designed with 30 participants in 2 different conditions. This design was used over repeated measures even though it requires a larger sample size in order to prevent demand characteristics, as in repeated measures the participants could learn the aim of the study. Independent samples also allow for avoiding order effects such as practice, as only one standardized list of words were used so the recall would likely increase with practice. Though, an independent measures design has limitations as variations within participants such as English proficiency which, even though was high in all participants could vary from 1 condition to the other leading to false conclusions.

The experiment had high reliability due to high replicability. As all instructions and materials presented in this experiment were standardized along with the order of occurrences for each participant in the study were conducted in a standardized manner. However, this experiment faced low ecological validity due to mundane realism as remembering a list of words from a video is artificial.

While the sample used was relevant as all participants were part of the IBDP allowing for easy application of the results to the context of highschool students. The internationality of the participants and thus different cultural backgrounds could lead to different understandings of the presented list affecting memory.

Some of the limitations of the experiment could have been countered with small modifications. The following changes can be made to do this. Initially ecological validity would be increased by reducing the mundane realism of the list of words used and removing any signs of small insignificant relationships.The list of words for example, while still being one syllable, can be associated to recent, school related events, thus reducing mundane realism. The problem with participant variability due to small differences in English proficiency could be counteracted by changing the sample set to only contain students taking English A as a language in the IBDP.

In conclusion, it can be seen that a 30 second delay between presentation and recall of a list of words will lead to significantly lowered recall of the last 5 words from the displayed list (recency effect) as compared to the no delay condition.

BIBLIOGRAPHY + APPENDICES OMITTED

6. EXAMPLE SIX (19/22)

Name: Investigation on the Effects of Verbal Interference in the Working Memory Model

Author: Anonymous

Session: May 2022

Level: SL

Contents

1. Introduction — 3
    a. Independent and dependent variables
    b. Null hypothesis
    c. Research Hypothesis

2. Exploration — 5
    a. Design
    b. Sampling and Participant Selection
    c. Controlled variables
    d. Materials

3. Analysis — 6
    a. Results
    b. Graph
    c. Inferential Statistics

4. Evaluation — 8
    a. Discussion
    b. Strengths and weaknesses
    c. Conclusion

5. References — 11
6. Appendices — 12

1. INTRODUCTION

It is well known that distractions such as music and noise during studying can make it harder for students to remember what they are studying into lasting memory. The investigation aims to understand the role of the phonological loop in Baddeley's Multimodal Working Memory Model which describes the processing of short-term memory models. The Working Memory Model proposes a more complicated visualization that includes more than one system for different types of information to be processed into short-term memory. The day-to-day has changed to the constant interference of technology that can often create obstruction of cognitive function.

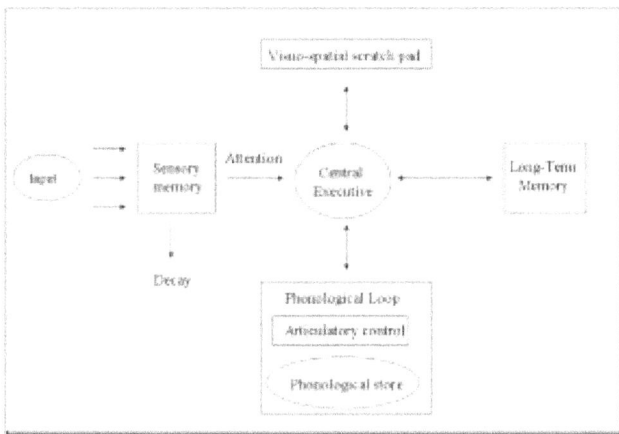

Image 1. Baddeley's Multimodal Working Memory Model

Image 1 shows the Working Memory Model by Baddeley and Hitch in 1974. Baddeley describes the central executive metaphorically as the company boss. The central executive can be described as the component that drives the memory system and allocates information to either the Visuospatial sketchpad, or the Phonological loop. (Mcleod, 2012) As mentioned earlier, the aim of the study was to explore the role of the Phonological loop in working memory, which stores auditory and articulatory based information.

A study performed by Salamé and Baddley in 1989 aimed to investigate the role of background music while actively memorizing information, specifically a number sequence. It was divided into three separate experiments: the first one tested the effects of quiet and exclusively instrumental music played, the second played vocal music, while the third, being the control, played no music. Participants were then asked to recall the numbers that they had been told to memorize during the experiment. It was found that the influence of music, both instrumental and vocal, had a significant effect on the ability to recall the number sequence accurately. However, the vocal music had a more significant effect.

Thus, the results of the study by Salamé and Baddley demanded more investigation into the hindering effects of verbal interference on the ability to memorize, or encode, information such as a number sequence or a list of items. The aim of this study is to investigate the role of the phonological loop in memory, more specifically the effects of verbal interference on the ability to encode information in short-term memory. The relevance behind such investigation is due to the growing concern with optimal memory capacity and retention when considering studying and education. As society does benefit from a well-rounded and educated collective of people. Increasing the knowledge behind the best way to learn can help teachers and educators increase their quality of teaching and the students can better study.

IV and DV:

The independent variable can be described as the presence of verbal interference during active memorization. This will be tested in two groups, one with verbal interference and another without the presence of verbal interference.

While the dependent variable can be described as the number of correct words recalled from the list given. The quantity of correct recalled words will be measured from the number of words recalled from a list of grocery items given to the participants.

Null hypothesis (H_o):

The null hypothesis for such investigation is that the verbal interference applied to memorizing information will have no effect on the ability to recall the information attempted to encode.

Research hypothesis (H_a):

The research hypothesis, however, is that the verbal interference in the experimental group will have a more significant effect on the serial recall of the items on the list given to the participants than the control group.

2. EXPLORATION

a. Design

This study used an independent measures design, meaning that all the participants were asked to participate once in the experiment all in all. This was chosen because it avoids order effects such as practice effects, which would allow participants more time to memorize the list provided to them. It avoids fatigue from the participants if they only have to participate in one experiment group with one single independent variable being tested on them. Also, the use of independent measures ensures that the participants do not recognize the aim of the study, which would hinder accurate results. The aim of the study is disguised as a control variable for participant expectancy.

b. Sampling and Participant Selection

The study consisted of opportunity sampling; such that students from the same high school grade were given the opportunity to participate in the study as it was efficient in the school setting. Important to note though, that the students that partook in psychology class were rejected from participating in the study as it would facilitate participants being aware of the aim of the study. That would affect the response to the experiment. The sampling resulted in 9 participants in the control group and 9 participants in the experimental group organized in a total of 18 participants for the entirety of the study.

The participants were to be allocated randomly in a group and given a list to memorize by reading it for 7 seconds. The list consisted of 10 grocery items, all written in the same font and size on a white sheet of paper. After they read it, they were asked to wait 7 seconds until they performed a written recall on a blank sheet of paper for 20 seconds. (see appendix e.) This method controls for researcher bias as well as controlling for participant variability, ensuring that there are no more similarities in one group than in another collectively. Researcher bias would hinder results if the groups were assigned purposefully as it would ensure biased results based on a categorization of participants. In the study, the participants were randomly divided into groups.

c. Control Variables

For both groups of participants, the same list with identical items was provided and with the same font and sizing. Creating identical lists, it eliminates the extraneous variable, such that the list is not a conflicting factor with the tasks asked of the participants. Furthermore, the procedure was conducted by the same people and in the same room for both groups.

The participants chosen were all from the same grade, which ensured similarities amongst all of them including language (English), socioeconomic status, and age. Thus ensuring that all the participants were able to memorize the items on the list with equal English fluency. Further, the time given to both groups was equal and fair to extirpate any form of advantage to either group as a result of more time to memorize the items on the lists.

d. Materials

As the items on the list were food items, they were chosen so as to be commonly known and recognized to not avoid memorization hindering due to lack of understanding of the word in some participants. Further, the materials were given on a blank sheet of paper with simple fonts and visible sizing. (See appendices)

3. ANALYSIS

a. Results

The results showed that the group with the influence of verbal interference performed significantly worse in recalling the words on the list. The group (control) with no verbal interference, when attempting to memorize the items, had a mean correct recall of words of 7.1 out of the total 10: 71.0% correct recall. While the group (experimental) had a mean correct recall of words of 4.78 out of the total 10: 47.8% correct recall. This demonstrates a certain possible effect of verbal interference on memory recall.

As can be seen on the graph below (Graph 1), there was a difference in correct recall suggesting a negative correlation between the level of recall and the application of verbal interference during active memorization.

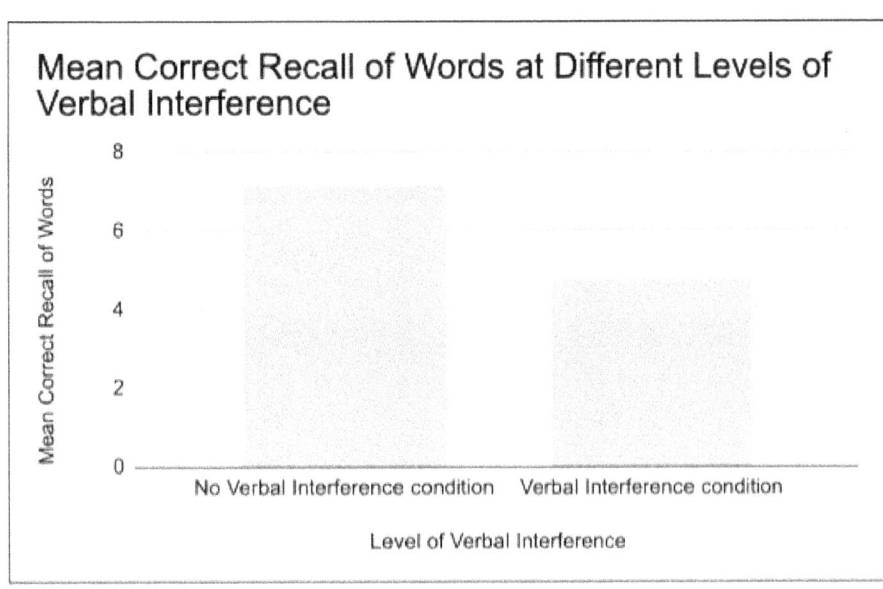

Graph 1.

Below, are the mean results of the number of correct recall words out of 10 for each group, as well as the percentage and the standard deviation per group.

	No Verbal Interference	Verbal Interference
Mean Results of correct recall out of 10	7.11	4.78
Percentage of correct recall	71.1%	47.8%
Standard Deviation	0.928	1.56

Table 1.

b. Inferential Statistics

Significance of data was obtained by performing the Mann Whitney Test to compare p-value and determine significance of the data. This test created a comparison of our data to evaluate significance determined by the p-value. The level of statistical significance for a Mann Whitney test is $p < 0.05$. The critical value of U at $p < 0.05$ is 21. Our results concluded a

U-value of 16.5. Therefore, the result was considered to be statistically significant. Moreover, the p-value provided by the Mann Whitney test was $P_1= 0.0018$, which falls under the value of significance being $p < 0.05$. This test of significance shows that the data is not statistically random and that the dependent variable is affected by the independent variable.

The significance of the data confirmed by the Mann Whitney test allows the rejection of the null hypothesis which was: the verbal interference applied to memorizing information will have no effect on the ability to recall the information attempted to encode. This means, however, that the research hypothesis be accepted. The research hypothesis, which was that the verbal interference in the experimental group will have a more significant effect on the serial recall of the items on the list given to the participants than the control group, and thus, as it was supported by the data, it be retained.

4. EVALUATION

a. Discussion

The phonological loop in Baddeley's Multimodal Working Memory Model is explored in the study conducted by Salamé and Baddeley in 1989. It was aimed to explore non-speechlike disruptions on phonological short-term stores. The results of the 1989 study are similar to the study conducted aimed to investigate the effect of verbal interference.

b. Strengths

The strengths of the procedure include several measures that ensured the extirpation of extraneous variables that would otherwise hinder accurate results. One strength of the procedure is that the same list was used for both groups, which created an equal difficulty level of memorization for both. This was able to ensure that the results were as accurate as possible, as well as reliable, due to the fact that there was no advantage given to one group hindering recall results.

The design was strong because the independent sample design ensured that the participants did not perform in more than one experiment. This is a strength for the study because it avoids order effects: the practice effect was avoided as the participants were not able to increase performance after the first experiment due to practice. The design was also strong because, as the participants only took part in one experiment, it reduced the chances of participant expectancy: such that they would not discover the aim of the study or work out the goal from patterns.

In the sampling, there were strengths because all of the participants were randomly allocated which reduces the chance of researcher bias and does not allow for hindered results. Further, all of the students were from the same grade and thus consist of the same cognitive abilities. The participants were all students from the same socioeconomic class, age group, school, education level, and all share English as a fluent language as the school is international. This made sure that all participants had a starting base level that did not give an advantage to certain individuals.

c. Limitations

The limitations of this study lie in the procedures, sampling and the design. The limitation of the sampling was that there was participant variability. This is due to, though very similar participants in the same grade, they all had different cognitive abilities in memory. It is to be noted that as the study was not an experiment null of extraneous variables, it was not able to control for initial memory abilities. This lowered the validity of the results as it did not allow all participants to begin the study with the same memorization abilities. Further limitations to the study are that the participants were not entirely random as they were close contacts to us and they went to the same school, it proposed more pressure on the participants to perform well. This added social pressure of being studied by upperclassmen might have hindered the results of the study.

There were limitations in this study within the procedure. In the consent form and information given prior to the study being conducted; many participants could have been able to discover the aim of the study as we had described the study as a test of memory and we played audio. All in all, the participants may have been subject to expectancy as they were told to memorize a set of words and later recall them within a time limit.

To obtain more accurate results, the limitations of the study require modifications. Some of which include, randomly choosing the participants to be in a group of students that are not associated with the researchers at all. The participants had they never met each other or gone to school with the researchers, would feel less pressure to perform well and as a result of feeling more relaxed would have performed better and more accurately.

Conclusion

On the whole, the null hypothesis (H_0) is to be rejected as it proposed that there would be no influence of verbal interference on the accuracy of recall and the data suggested otherwise. Consequently, the research hypothesis (H_1) is accepted as it proposed that there would be a negative correlation between the independent and dependent variables. Meaning that the data suggests that there is a negative correlation between the degree of verbal interference and the accuracy of recall supporting the role of the Phonological Loop in the Working Memory Model.

BIBLIOGRAPHY + APPENDICES OMITTED

7. EXAMPLE SEVEN (22/22)

Name: An investigation into the theory of reconstructive memory

Author: Anonymous

Session: May 2021

Level: SL

TABLE OF CONTENTS

Introduction 1

Exploration 3

    Design 3

    Sampling 3

    Procedure and Materials 4

    Control Variables 4

Analysis 5

    Descriptive Statistics 5

    Inferential Statistics 6

Evaluation 7

References 9

Appendices 10

    Appendix A: Standardised instructions 10

    Appendix B: Informed consent 11

    Appendix C: Debriefing 12

    Appendix D: Car crash video 12

    Appendix E: Questionnaire A 13

    Appendix F: Questionnaire B 14

    Appendix G: Raw data and descriptive statistics calculation 15

    Appendix H: Inferential statistics calculation 16

INTRODUCTION

Cognitive psychologists believe that memory is a crucial cognitive process. It refers to how we encode, store and retrieve information. However, are these memories accurate records of the past, or can they become contaminated? Bartlett (1932) uses the theory of Reconstructive Memory to argue that memory is influenced by external, or post-event information, such that it is reconstructed i.e. it is recreated through past events as opposed to simply being retrieved when needed. In other words, remembering is considered to be an active process in which we try to make sense of our surroundings through the use of pre-existing information, perhaps leading to distorted memories. This pre-existing information could be stored in 'schemas': stable, deeply rooted mental representations that influence our beliefs and expectations (Popov, 2018). We rely on schemas in order to simplify the world and create heuristics (mental shortcuts) which aid our thinking.

Loftus and Palmer (1974) conducted a lab experiment to investigate the extent to which such post-event information could affect participants' memory, and whether these memories had been reconstructed or not. 45 students from the University of Washington were asked to watch videos of traffic accidents followed by a questionnaire about the events. The post-event information was disguised as a change of wording in a "leading" question which asked the participants "About how fast were the cars going when they hit each other?". Four other conditions were used where the verb "hit" was replaced with either "smashed", "collided", "bumped" or "contacted". The sample followed an independent measures design such that each of the five groups contained only 9 participants. The findings showed that participants provided higher speed estimates when more 'emotionally intense' verbs were used. For instance, those who read the verb "smashed" reported a mean estimate of 40.5 mph, whereas those who read the verb "hit" reported a lower mean estimate of 34.0 mph. This is due to the belief that the impact perceived of an accident is gentler for 'hit' than for 'smashed'. As such, we could see that participants' memory (measured through speed estimates) of the car crash had been reconstructed as a result of a set of pre-existing schemas that certain verbs infer greater emotional intensities than others. This allows us to conclude that reconstructed memories lack accuracy, thus raising concerns regarding the reliability of memory.

This present investigation seeks to investigate the theory of reconstructive memory by partially replicating Loftus and Palmer's experiment. Instead of five conditions, two independent groups of participants will be used and given the leading question using the verbs 'hit' and 'smashed'. Our experiment aims to investigate how post-event information affects memory recall of a car crash. This aim is relevant because it sheds light upon current, topical psychological and legal issues such as the reliability of eyewitness testimonies. In Loftus and Palmer's experiment, the results indicated that participants in an eyewitness situation provided inaccurate and contradictory speed estimates, thus suggesting the possibility of unreliable reconstructed memories. As such, by conducting this experiment, we are hoping to gain a better understanding regarding the reliability of memory in such situations. Our prediction is that post-event information will indeed influence the memories of a car crash, causing them to be reconstructed, possibly through the reliance upon schemas.

IV: The emotional intensity of the verb ('hit' or 'smashed') used in the leading question.
DV: Speed estimates (km/h) provided by participants.

Research Hypothesis (one-tailed): Participants who are asked the leading question with the verb 'smashed' will report higher speed estimates than participants who are asked the question with the verb 'hit'.

Null Hypothesis: There will be no significant difference between the speed estimates in both groups.

EXPLORATION

Design

The experiment used an independent measures design, such that different participants were in each condition, preventing their responses from being susceptible to order effects. This means that since each group only answered one questionnaire, the participants did not get tired and were not able to practice answering the questions, preventing demand characteristics i.e. it was unlikely to guess the aim of the experiment and provide speed estimates which the researchers were expecting. Furthermore, the participants were randomly allocated into each condition; upon entering the classroom, they were asked to sit anywhere they want. The different questionnaires were randomly placed on the desks such that neither the researchers nor participants knew which table had which questionnaire, hence random allocation.

Sampling

Participants were selected using opportunity sampling, as this was easy and convenient to do in a school setting, however there was an exclusion criterion of psychology students as this could have resulted in demand characteristics; it is more likely that psychology students have learned about Loftus and Palmer's experiment, in which case they would have provided biased speed estimates. The sampling resulted in 24 (13 males, 11 females) 16-year old non-psychology IGCSE students. Our school is international therefore the participants were ethnically mixed from different cultural backgrounds and had a high level of proficiency in English. Their age allowed them to sign their informed consent while their English proficiency prevented language from being an extraneous variable.

Procedure and Materials

The participants were asked to be at a specified classroom during afternoon registration. The classroom was chosen such that it was large enough to accommodate 24 participants. The desks were arranged in exam conditions with each having a questionnaire and a pen. After the participants were seated, the standardized instructions were read (Appendix A), asking them to read and sign their informed consent (Appendix B). As the instructions were being read, the other researchers collected the consent forms. Participants were asked not to write their names on the questionnaires, reserving their confidentiality and ensuring ethical considerations were met. After the car crash video was played (Appendix D), the participants turned over the questionnaires (Appendices E and F) and started answering in silence. This particular video was chosen as it was short (10 seconds) and the crash displayed an appropriate level of violence such that the emotional intensity of the verbs 'smashed' and 'hit' would have (potentially) had a contextually appropriate effect on the speed estimates provided. Upon completion of their questionnaires, participants were debriefed (Appendix C) and then they left.

Control Variables

Both questionnaires used the same font (Times New Roman pt.12), had an identical format and asked the same questions (except the change in the verb), thus negating the impact of these extraneous variables and making the two conditions controlled. The standardised instructions and debrief were read by the same person, therefore clarity of speech was not affected, and the video was displayed on a large board such that all participants could clearly see the car crash with ease. Furthermore, the participants were the same age and presumably had no driving experience, mitigating the effects of individual differences that could have potentially affected the speed estimates.

ANALYSIS

Descriptive Statistics

The data obtained was at least ordinal. As such, the means and standard deviations (SD) were calculated from the raw data (Appendix G), since they are appropriate measures for the analysis of interval data. Group A ('hit') estimated a mean speed of 60.7 km/h, with a SD of 11.7 km/h; whereas group B ('smashed') estimated a mean speed of 73.2 km/h, with a SD of 18.1 km/h. This data is summarised in the figure below. It is important to note that in calculating these statistics, two values have been identified as outliers and excluded from the calculations, since they did not fit within the general trend and were contextually inappropriate, and thus could have impacted the interpretation of the statistics. These values are '5' from group A and '6' from group B. Therefore, only 11 participants from each condition have been analysed.

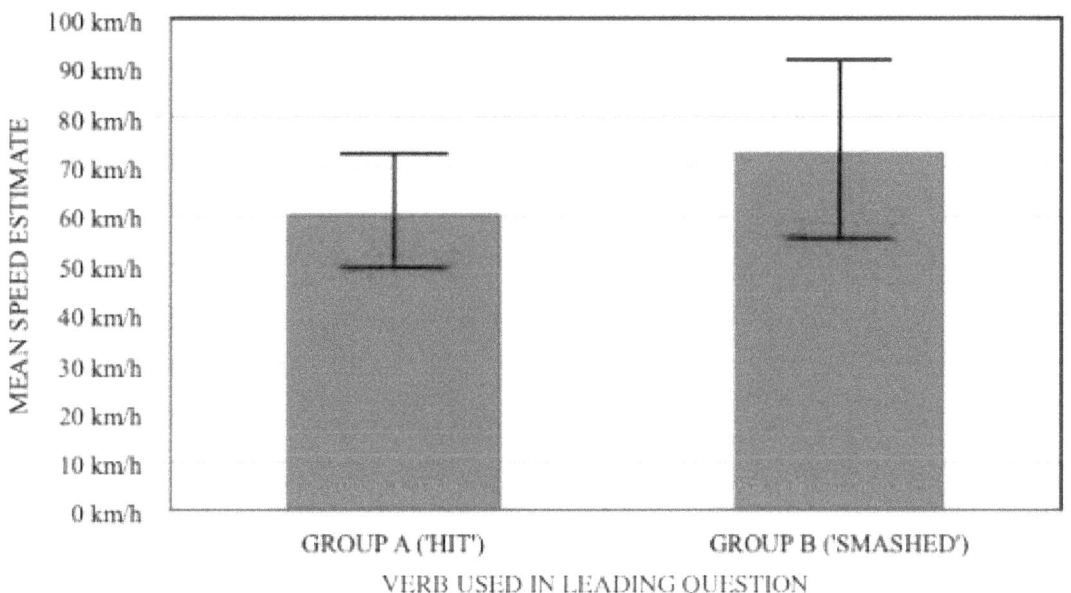

Bar chart showing the differences in the mean (±standard deviation) speed estimates between Group A ('hit') and Group B ('smashed')

Created using: https://www.meta-chart.com/bar

The mean speed of Group B was 12.5 km/h higher than that of group A. The SDs showed moderate spread around the mean for both groups, although the SD for group B was 55% higher than group A, suggesting that there was greater variability in the data and greater disagreement amongst participants about the car speed. In the original experiment, the difference in speed estimates between 'hit' and 'smashed' was 10.5 km/h (Loftus and Palmer, 1974), which is similar to our difference of 12.5 km/h. As such, our results agree quantitatively. At first glance, this descriptive data seems to support the research hypothesis that there is causality between the emotional intensity of the verb and the mean speed estimates; however, inferential statistics are required to confirm this.

Inferential Statistics

The Mann-Whitney U-test of statistical significance was applied for the inferential analysis, as our experiment employed an independent measures design. Furthermore, the data acquired deviated from normality and the sample size was quite small, therefore a parametric test would have not been appropriate. The test indicated that the speed estimates in group B (mean rank = 13.95) were significantly higher than the speed estimates in group A (mean rank = 9.05); $U(11, 11) = 33.5$, $p < 0.05$, one-tailed (see Appendix H). The calculated U-value was less than the critical value of 34, thus making the results statistically significant. That is to say that post-event information, through the use of different emotional intensity verbs in the leading questions, did indeed affect memory recall. In other words, the null hypothesis is rejected, and the research hypothesis is accepted, due to the results being of statistical significance, i.e. the probability of this being a coincidence is less than 5%.

EVALUATION

The theory of Reconstructive Memory could be used to explain our findings. According to the theory, the participants initially perceived the car crash similarly; however, upon receiving new information in the questionnaires, their memories of the car crash were reconstructed based on the implications associated with the verbs in the leading question. This misinformation effect is a source of problematic discussion amongst psychologists, as it alludes to the idea that our memories are unreliable, and hence, as aforementioned, raises concerns about events like eyewitness testimonies, where people are unwittingly being deceived by their memories.

A strength of our opportunity sample is that it contained 13 males and 11 females, representative of the gender proportion in our schools' IGCSE students, ensuring high population validity. However, due to the participants' age, they were not eligible for a driving license (legal age is 18), which is problematic because the questionnaires required them to answer a question associated with driving; something which they (probably) did not have much experience with. This means that they would have not been strongly familiar with certain speeds; they could have had a lack of schema regarding what 60km/h would visually look like in a real-life crash. Using 18-year old IB students as part of our sample would be a good modification because they are likely to have had some experience with driving, thus mitigating this limitation.

A strength of our procedure is that many extraneous variables were controlled. The fact that the classroom, questionnaires and video length were kept the same ensured that participants were treated equally. As such, their speed estimates were unlikely to be biased as a result of confounding variables such as environmental setting. However, a limitation of the procedure is that the questionnaires failed to explicitly request a unit to be accompanied with the speed estimate. Some participants gave their answer in km/h while one gave it in mph, however, the majority did not provide any unit. This meant that their intentions were unknown, and therefore had to be interpreted as km/h, since that is the conventional unit. Originally, we planned not to request a specific unit due to the different backgrounds of the participants and thus did not want to restrict their choice so that they could provide the speed using a unit they're familiar with. Simply adding a note at the end of the question such as "please specify your unit" would be a useful modification as it would ensure that there is no confusion for the participants when answering and for the researchers when analysing.

Finally, a strength of the independent measures design is that it prevented participants from guessing the aim and consequently from displaying demand characteristics. If the design was repeated measures, participants would have been familiar with the questions and could have noticed the change in verbs, thus introducing a confounding variable. As a limitation of the design, randomly allocating participants to groups meant that participants' variability was not accounted for. Although none of the participants had their driving licenses, some could have been more familiar with car speeds than others, perhaps as a result of playing racing video games or watching car races, therefore they could have provided more realistic estimates due to their increased exposure to cars and their (presumably) greater understanding of speeds. A modification would be to allocate participants to groups as matched pairs based on video game experience, ensuring that this potentially confounding variable would be equally distributed amongst the two groups, reducing individual differences between participants.

In conclusion, our experiment was shown to be of statistical significance at the $p \leq 0.05$ level, supporting the theory of reconstructive memory. However, applying the modifications aforementioned may enhance the degree of causation and increase our certainty in the results.

BIBLIOGRAPHY + APPENDICES OMITTED

www.ingramcontent.com/pod-product-compliance
Lightning Source LLC
Chambersburg PA
CBHW042019090526
44590CB00029B/4335